MUHAMMAD ALI

THE FINAL VICTORY

COPYRIGHT 2016 PAUL LEO FASO
ALL RIGHTS RESERVED

ISBN
978-1-943529-32-2
ANY AND ALL ADDITIONAL SOURCES TO INCLUDE
ARTICLES, QUOTES, VIDEO IMAGE STILLS ARE
UTILIZED UNDER FAIR RIGHTS USE 17U.S.V.SECTION 107

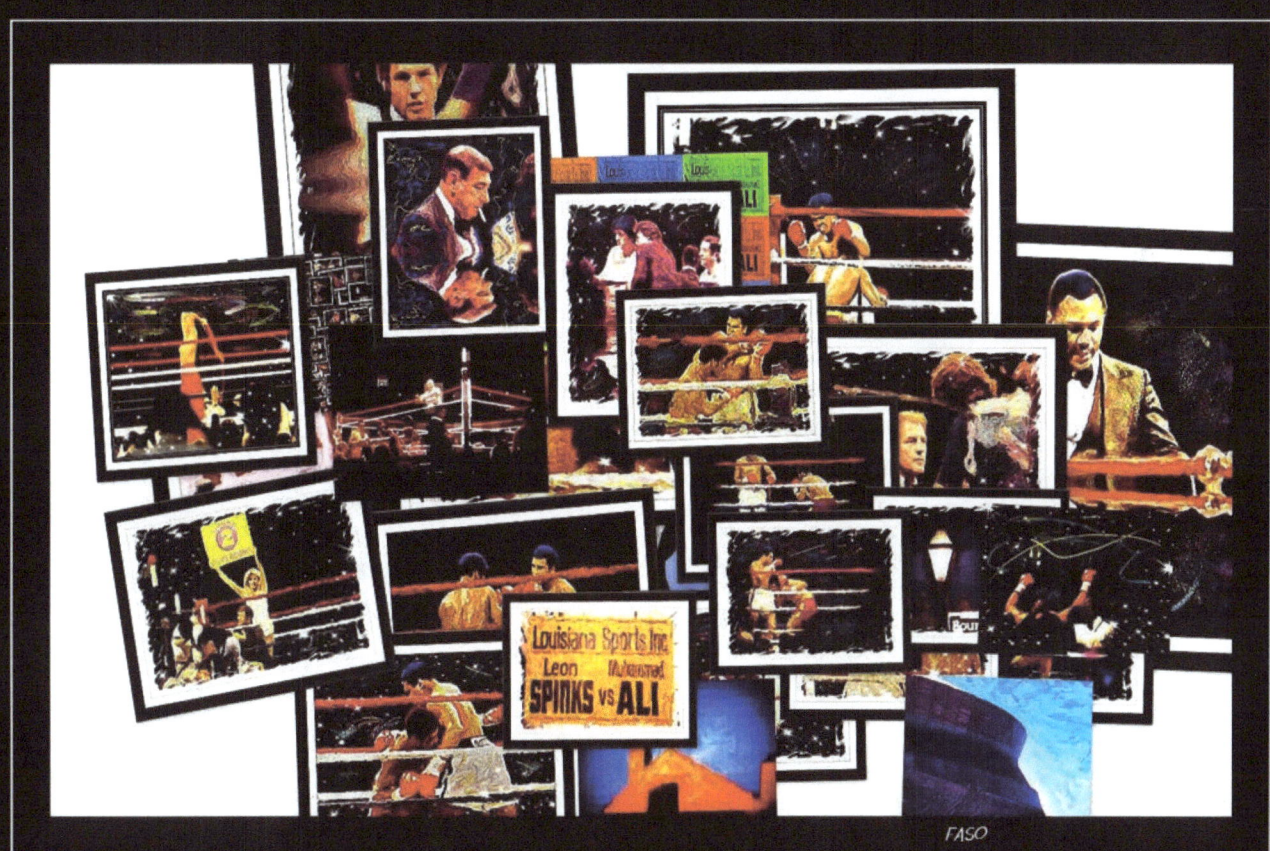

MUHAMMAD ALI

THE FINAL VICTORY

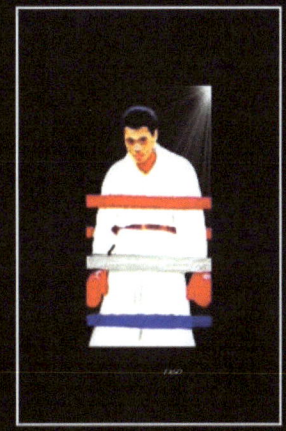

"THE KID DID WITH HIS LIFE WHAT HE WANTED TO DO, AND GETS MORE OUT OF A WINK AND SMILE THAN WE DO OUT OF A WHOLE CONVERSATION."
-ANGELO DUNDEE-

MUHAMMAD ALI'S LIFE LONG TRAINER

Louisiana Sports, Inc.

Leon SPINKS vs **Muhammad ALI**

FASO

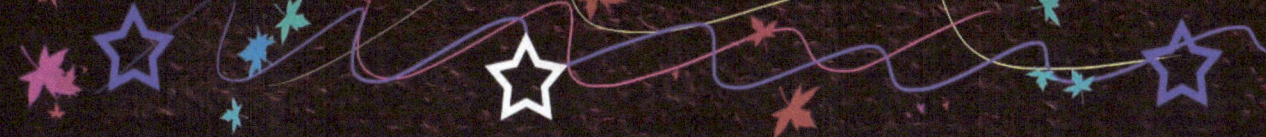

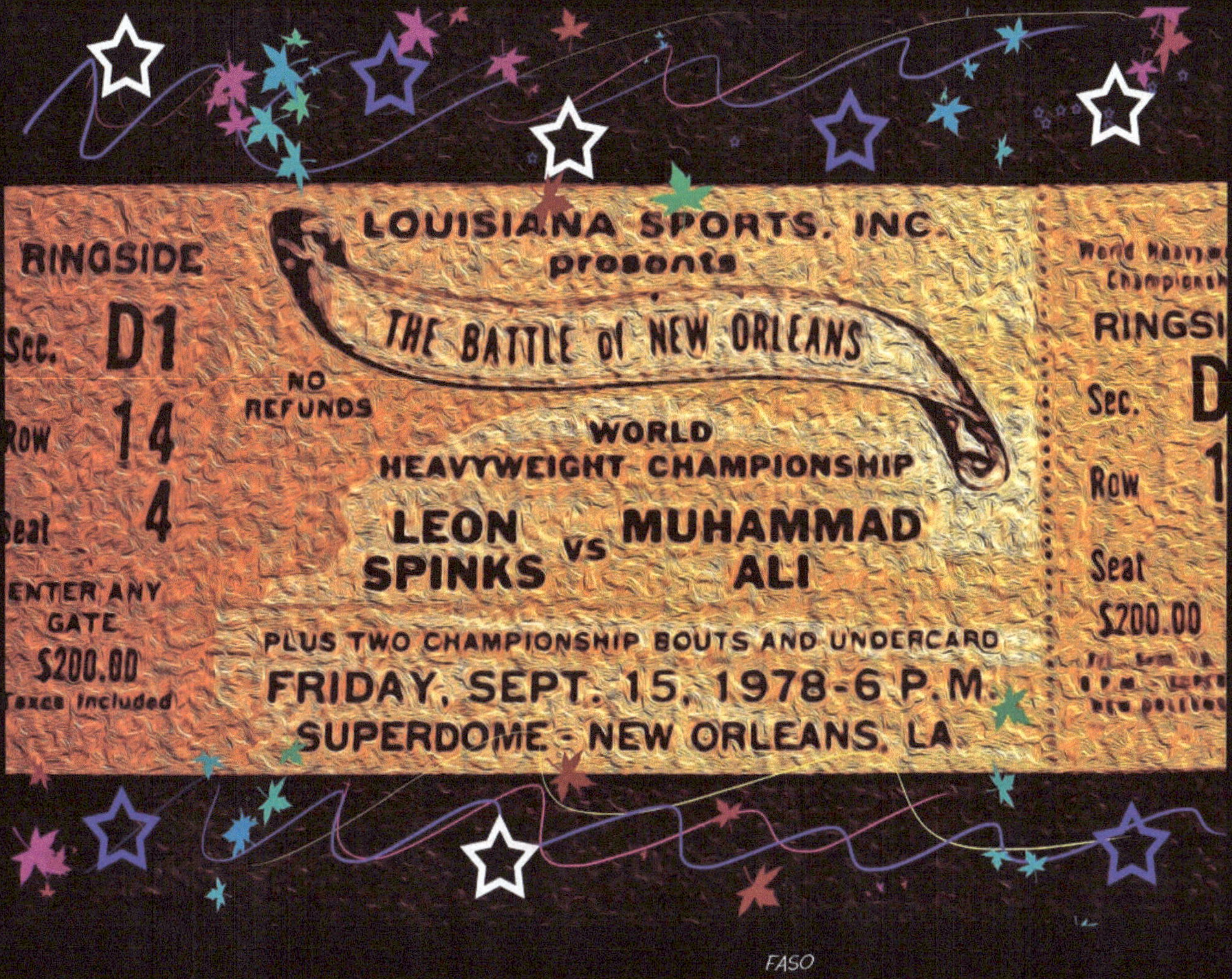

RINGSIDE
Sec. D1
Row 14
Seat 4
ENTER ANY GATE
$200.00
Taxes included
NO REFUNDS
LOUISIANA SPORTS, INC
presents
THE BATTLE OF NEW ORLEANS
WORLD HEAVYWEIGHT CHAMPIONSHIP
LEON SPINKS vs MUHAMMAD ALI
PLUS TWO CHAMPIONSHIP BOUTS AND UNDERCARD
FRIDAY, SEPT. 15, 1978-6 P.M.
SUPERDOME - NEW ORLEANS, LA
Sec.
Row
Seat
$200.00
FASO

DEDICATION

FASO

THIS BOOK IS DEDICATED TO THE EVERLASTING BROTHERHOOD OF
MUHAMMAD ALI AND HOWARD COSELL.
THROUGHOUT THEIR LIFETIMES, THEY LEFT TO THE WORLD AN EXAMPLE
OF WHAT MUTUAL RESPECT AND HONOR BETWEEN MEN SHOULD ALWAYS BE.

"MOVE THE WORLD"

"LET HIM WHO WOULD MOVE THE WORLD...
FIRST MOVE HIMSELF."
-SOCRATES-

INTRODUCTION

ON SEPTEMBER 15, 1978, I ARRIVED AT THE SUPERDOME IN NEW ORLEANS, MY SECOND VISIT TO THE CITY AND MY FIRST VIEW OF THE INTERIOR OF THE DOME. THERE IS A GOOD REASON WHY IT IS CALLED THE SUPERDOME. IT IS HUGE IN EVERY WAY. THE MOST IMPORTANT FUNCTION OF THE SIZE OF THE SUPERDOME WAS TO HOLD THE ENORMOUS CROWD THAT EVENING FOR ONE OF THE GREATEST SPORTING FIGURES OF MODERN HISTORY…MUHAMMAD ALI.

ALREADY A SUPERSTAR, WITH A RICH HISTORY OF POLITICAL, SOCIAL AND BOXING BATTLES UNDER HIS BELT, ALI ENTERED THE RING WITH THE CLEAR INTENSION OF RECLAIMING, FOR THE THIRD TIME, THE HEAVYWEIGHT BOXING CHAMPIONSHIP OF THE WORLD. MUHAMMAD ALI WOULD ALSO TRANSFORM HIMSELF THAT EVENING INTO A LIVING LEGEND.
A MASSIVE CROWD OF 70,000 PEOPLE FILLED THE SUPERDOME, WITH AN ESTIMATED 90 MILLION GLOBAL TELEVISION VIEWERS, POISED TO WITNESS THIS HISTORIC EVENT.
IN LESS THAN ONE HOUR, THE WORLD WOULD COME TO SEE THE FINAL VICTORY OF THE GREATEST FIGHTER EVER TO WEAR THE HEAVYWEIGHT CHAMPIONSHIP BELT. FOR A RECORD THIRD TIME.
WHEN THE 15TH ROUND ENDED, THE JUDGES AND THE REFEREE AWARDED THE UNANIMOUS DECISION TO THE VICTOR, MUHAMMAD ALI.
THIS SERIES OF PHOTOGRAPHS ARE A SMALL PART OF THAT NIGHT. THEY REPRESENT MY EFFORT TO CAPTURE SOME OF THE EVENTS THAT TOOK PLACE INSIDE THE SUPERDOME, NOT ONLY DURING THE FIGHT, BUT THOSE MAGICAL MOMENTS BEFORE AND AFTER THE LAST ROUND.

THE 15 ROUND FIGHT WAS DIFFICULT FOR ALI AT 36 YEARS OF AGE AND WAS TELLING AFTER THE FINAL BELL, WHEN THE FIRST TO CLIMB INTO THE RING WAS ALI'S LIFELONG TRAINER, ANGELO DUNDEE. THIS WAS THE LAST PUBLIC MOMENT OF VICTORY FOR THE NOW LEGENDARY CHAMPION, BUT ALI LOOKED INTO THE EYES OF DUNDEE TO CONFIRM THE AWAITING DECISION. THAT PHOTOGRAPH TELLS THE STORY OF THIS FIGHT. THE FIGHT WENT THE DISTANCE AND WAS LEFT FOR THE JUDGES AND REFEREE TO DECIDE; THERE WERE NO STUNNING KNOCK DOWNS OR OVERWHELMING ROUNDS, BUT RATHER A METHODICAL BOXING EXHIBITION PUT ON BY A MASTER. A SOLID OFFENCE THAT TOOK BACK FROM LEON SPINKS THE CHAMPIONS CROWN THAT NEVER SEEMED TO FIT HIM PROPERLY.

JUDGING BY THE THUNDEROUS CROWD ERUPTION JUST AFTER THE BELL, IT WAS ALL FOR ALI. WHEN THE FINAL DECISION WAS ANNOUNCED, THERE WAS A WAVE OF HUMANITY THAT SURGED FORWARD, SURROUNDED THE RING, OVERWHELMED SECURITY, THEN SWEPT AN EXUBERANT MUHAMMAD ALI OFF OF HIS FEET AND CARRIED HIM OUT FOREVER INTO HISTORY.

THOSE ARE THE MOMENTS I WILL ALWAYS REMEMBER AND I LEAVE THIS BOOK OF STYLIZED PHOTOGRAPHIC ART AS WITNESS TO WHAT HAPPENED THAT SPECIAL NIGHT IN NEW ORLEANS.

PAUL LEO FASO

TECHNICAL CHALLENGES

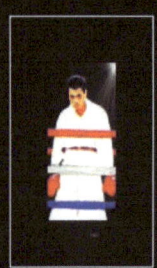

TO GIVE YOU AN IDEA OF WHAT THE TECHNICAL CHALLENGES WERE AT THE TIME, IS ESSENTIAL TO REMEMBER THIS WAS 1978; PRE DIGITAL, NON COMPUTER CHIP CAMERA DAYS, WHEN 35mm FILM WAS KING AND CAMERAS WERE NOT EASILY OPERATED IN LOW LIGHT ARENAS.

I USED TWO NIKON CAMERAS, ONE A NEW "EL" WITH AN AUTO EXPOSURE SETTER. A FIXED TELEPHOTO LENS, 2.8 APERTURE, AND ANOTHER NIKON "F2", WITH A NORMAL 50mm FAST LENS. TO BOOST THE SHUTTER SPEED IN THE "EL" FOR THE FIGHT SCENES. I USED KODAK EKTACHROME HIGH SPEED COLOR FILM AND "PUSHED" THE I.S.A. FILM SPEED FROM A FACTORY 200 SETTING TO 400. DOUBLING ITS SENSITIVITY TO LIGHT AND LESSONING THE SHUTTER ON EXPOSURE, WHICH PREVENTED BLURRING OF THE MOTIONS OF THE FIGHTERS.

BECAUSE I CHOSE TO ROAM AROUND THE EVENT FOR A FULL RANGE OF IMAGERY, I LEFT MY RINGSIDE SEAT AND CHANGED PERSPECTIVE FROM OTHER PHOTOGRAPHERS WHO WERE IN CLASSIC FIXED POSITIONS ON THE RING APRON. THEIR SHOTS WERE ALL CLOSE, DIRECTED UPWARD AND MOSTLY HAD THAT SINGLE PERSPECTIVE, BY PLACING MYSELF SEVERAL FEET BACK FROM THE RING. I SHOT FULL AND LEVEL WITH A SHORT TELEPHOTO LENS THROUGH THE ROPES TO GAIN A STRAIGHT ON PERSPECTIVE. MOST OF THE OTHER CLOSE UPS OF THE MEDIA, CROWD AND OTHER ACTIVITIES WERE SHOT WITH THE "F2" AND KODACHROME.

ACKNOWLEDGMENTS

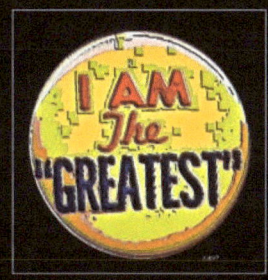

LIKE MILLIONS OF OTHER AMERICANS, I GREW UP WITH MUHAMMAD ALI. HIS WAS A FORCE THAT DOMINATED THE LATTER PARTS OF THE 20TH CENTURY. WHEN I BEGAN TO RESEARCH HIS IMPACT, I WAS STAGGERED BY THE DATA PROVIDED BY LINKED UNIVERSITY LIBRARIES ON MUHAMMAD ALI BOOKS, EBOOKS, PAPERS, THESIS/DISSERTATIONS, ARTICLES, FILMS, VIDEOS, & DVDS. SUFFICE TO SAY, WORLDCAT.COM BREAKS DOWN THE NUMBERS AS DOES AMAZON WITH A BLISTERING 81,140 SEARCH RESULTS THAT FILTER DOWN TO THE MOST DEFINITIVE EVIDENCE, YET SUPPORTING ALI'S CLAIM OF BEING "THE GREATEST", YOUTUBE POSTS OVER 100 MILLION VIEWS OF HIS FIGHTS ONLINE TODAY. SO, I HAVE TO ACKNOWLEDGE FIRST THE VERACITY OF MUHAMMAD ALI'S CLAIM AS "THE GREATEST". HE IS, HANDS DOWN, THE ONLY ONE IN THAT DRIVERS SEAT, AND WHAT'S MORE, THERE ISN'T ANYBODY...I MEAN ANYBODY...THAT'S EVEN CLOSE. MUHAMMAD ALI IS A PUBLISHING WONDER IN AND OF HIMSELF. FROM NORMAN MAILER'S "THE FIGHT" TO "G.O.A.T". "THE GREATEST OF ALL TIME". THE LARGEST BOOK PRINTED IN THE WORLD, 772 PAGES IN LIMITED EDITION (OVER 3000 IMAGES, BY 150 PHOTOGRAPHERS) AT $15,000.00 PER COPY BY PUBLISHING GIANT, TASCHEN. IN ALL, THOUSANDS UPON THOUSANDS OF BOOKS, ARTICLES, PAPERS WRITTEN AND PUBLISHED FROM ALL OVER THE WORLD ABOUT AN AMERICAN HEAVYWEIGHT BOXER WHO BECAME A LEGEND. QUITE A STUNNING ACKNOWLEDGMENT.
WITH THIS MONUMENTAL LEGACY IN MIND, "THE FINAL VICTORY" ENTERS THE FIELD, UNLIKE MANY OF THE SWEEPING VIEWS OF MUHAMMAD ALI'S LIFE, THIS BOOK STOPS THE CLOCK AND LOOKS AT ONE PIVOTAL HOUR OF ALI'S STORIED LIFE, WHERE MUHAMMAD ALI TRANSITIONED FROM A MERE MORTAL MAN TO AN UNCOMPROMISED LEGEND.
"THE FINAL VICTORY" WILL NOT BE THE LAST BOOK ABOUT MUHAMMAD ALI, BUT WILL ONLY ADD TO THE NEW CHAPTERS YET TO BE WRITTEN OF HIS ENDURING LEGACY.

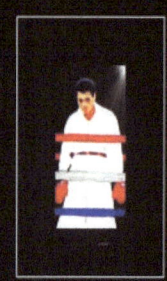

AUTHOR'S NOTE

THERE WERE SEVERAL WAYS TO ADD THE VARIOUS COMMENTS MADE BY MANY PEOPLE ABOUT MUHAMMAD ALI THROUGHOUT THIS BOOK. I HAVE MADE AN ATTEMPT TO INTERMINGLE THEM WITH THE ACTUAL QUOTES MUHAMMAD ALI MADE DURING HIS LIFETIME. THEN SURROUNDED THEM WITH A NUMBER OF OTHER QUOTES THAT WERE MADE RINGSIDE OF THE FIGHT ITSELF.
THIS FIGHT WAS MUHAMMAD ALI'S "FINAL VICTORY" IN EVERY WAY. TO LEAVE OUT THE ESSENCE OF THOSE KEY MOMENTS IN HIS LIFE WOULD BE TO MISS THE MOST IMPORTANT PART OF HIS BOXING CAREER.

PAUL LEO FASO

MUHAMMAD ALI

"HE IS HERCULES STRUGGLING THROUGH THE 12 LABORS, HE IS JASON CHASING THE GOLDEN FLEECE. HE IS GALAHAD, CYRANO, D'ARTAGNAN. WHEN HE SCOWLS, STRONG MEN SHUDDER, AND WHEN HE SMILES, WOMEN SWOON. THE MYSTERIES OF THE UNIVERSE ARE HIS TOYS. HE RATTLES THE THUNDER AND LOOSES THE LIGHTNING."
TIME MAGAZINE

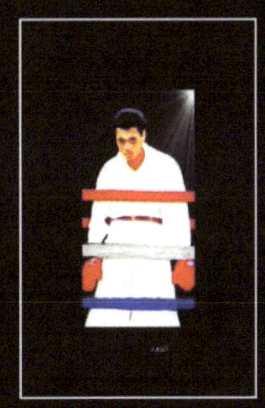

"TODAY FOOTBALL MAY HAVE ITS NAMATHS AND OTHER STARS,
BASKETBALL ITS CHAMBERLAINS, BIRDS, JORDANS,
BASEBALL HAS ITS BABE RUTHS, AND
BOXING HAS ITS CASSIUS CLAY.
BUT HUMANITY HAS MUHAMMAD ALI."
THOMAS MEEKER, PRESIDENT & CEO CHURCHILL DOWNS, INC.

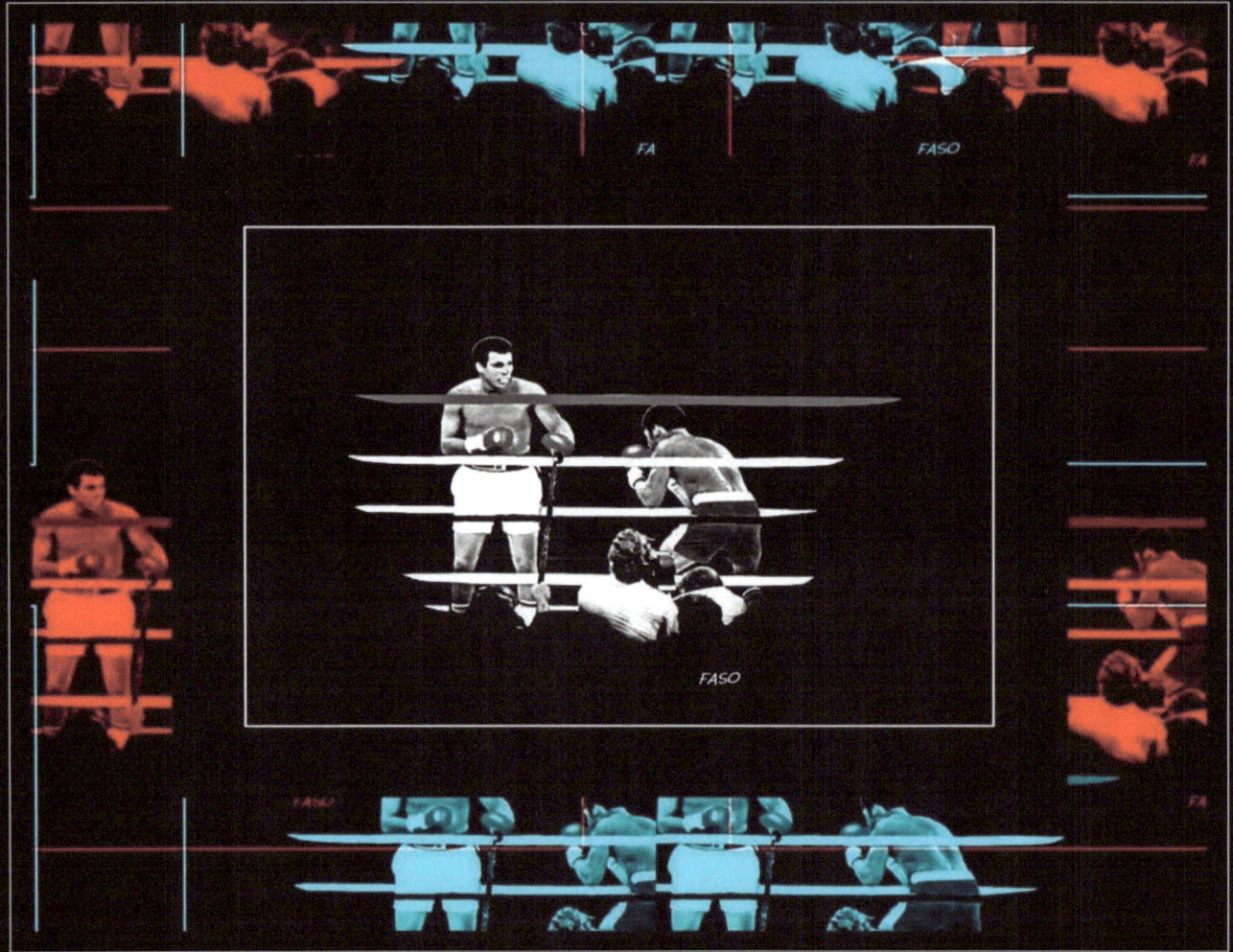

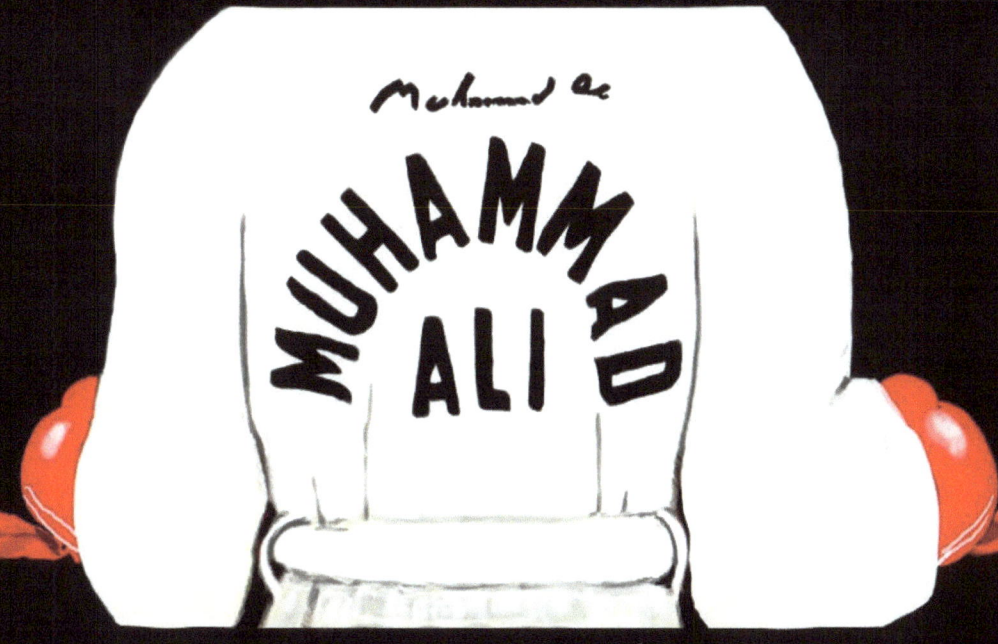

ABC Sports

FRANK GIFFORD   **HOWARD COSELL**   **CHRIS SCHENKEL**

"THAT'S WHERE HE LIVED"

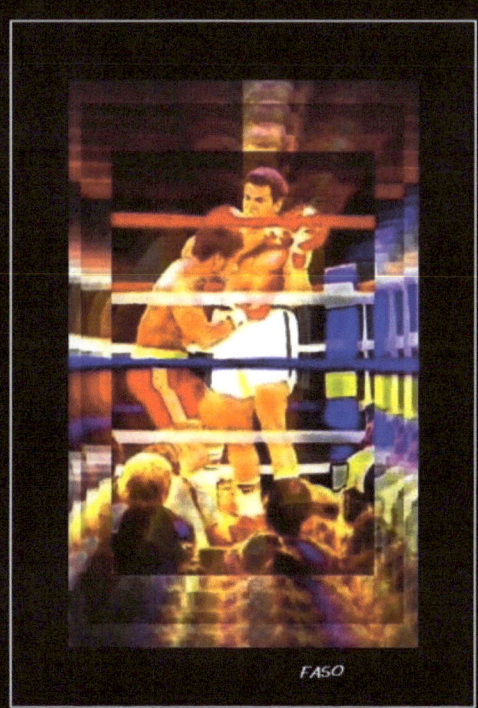

"I CAN TELL YOU, ALI SPENT ALL HIS TIME IN THE GYM.
THAT'S WHERE HE LIVED."
JIMMY ELLIS – HEAVYWEIGHT CHAMPION

"SOME OF THAT DISCIPLINE"

"ALI WAS A GUY THAT HAD A LOT OF DISCIPLINE, IF YOU HUNG AROUND HIM.
YOU'D BE ABLE TO GET SOME OF THE DISCIPLINE THAT HE HAD. I LEARNED FROM THAT.
HE WAS A SWEET MAN."
LARRY HOLMES – HEAVYWEIGHT CHAMPION

HOWARD COSELL
ABC SPORTS

"ONE OF THE BEST ONES OUT THERE WAS A GUY NAMED HOWARD COSELL, HE WAS THE BEST."
LARRY HOLMES – HEAVYWEIGHT CHAMPION

FRANK GIFFORD
ABC SPORTS

"TAKE THAT TRIP WITH MUHAMMAD ALI BECAUSE HE IS A TRIP ALTOGETHER."

COSELL SHINES

THROUGHOUT THE FIGHT, HOWARD COSELL GOES DEEP INTO MUHAMMAD ALI, THE MAN, THE MYTH, AND THE FIGHTER. TO MANY COSELL'S PROFESSIONALISM BROUGHT OUT ONE OF THE FINEST COMMENTARIES EVER DONE, LIVE, ON CAMERA.

"ATHLETE OF THE CENTURY"

"MUHAMMAD ALI, GREAT CHAMPION, ATHLETE OF THE CENTURY."
FRANK GIFFORD – ABC SPORTS – PRE-FIGHT INTERVIEW

"WE WILL NEVER SEE THE LIKES OF HIM AGAIN"

"HE IS EVERYTHING AN ATHLETE SHOULD BE AND A MAN SHOULD BE. WE WILL NEVER SEE THE LIKES OF HIM AGAIN AND I BASED APOLLO CREED ON HIM – THANK GOD A CHARACTER LIKE HIM EXISTED, BECAUSE I WOULD HAVE NEVER THOUGHT ONE UP." SYLVESTER STALLONE – AKA – "ROCKY"

"THAT'S ME EXACTLY"

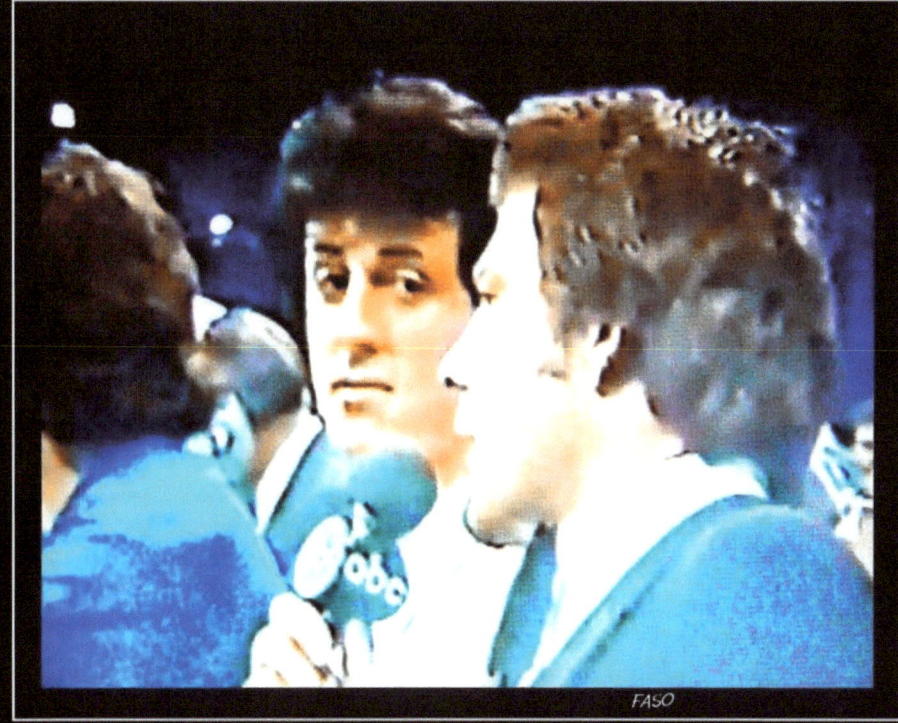

-WATCHING ROCKY II WITH MUHAMMAD ALI –
"HE WATCHED THE OPENING SCENES OF ROCKY II IN SILENCE, NOT SPEAKING UNTIL THE SCENE IN WHICH APOLLO CREED, THE HEAVYWEIGHT CHAMPION DELIVERS A TELEVISED CHALLENGE DESIGNED TO TAUNT ROCKY BACK INTO THE RING. "THAT'S ME, ALL RIGHT," ALI SAID. "APOLLO SOUNDS LIKE ME.. INSULTING THE OPPONENT IN THE PRESS TO GET HIM PSYCHED OUT. THAT'S ME EXACTLY."
ROGER EBERT – CHICAGO SUN-TIMES

"ROCKY"

"NOBODY IS GONNA HIT AS HARD AS LIFE, BUT IT AIN'T ABOUT HOW HARD YOU CAN HIT. IT'S ABOUT HOW HARD YOU CAN GET HIT AND KEEP MOVING FORWARD. HOW MUCH YOU CAN TAKE AND KEEP MOVING FORWARD. THIS IS HOW WINNING IS DONE."
"ROCKY" BALBOA
AKA
SYLVESTER STALLONE

"BOOM BOOM ROOM"

"ALL OF A SUDDEN THE SUPERDOME WAS A DIFFERENT KIND OF BOOM BOOM ROOM."
"BLOOD, SWEAT AND CHEERS" SPORTS ILLUSTRATED – SEPTEMBER 25, 1978

EDY WILLIAMS
FROM "THE LAST STARLET"
BY
ROGER EBERT

"WE'RE TALKING ABOUT THE GIRL WHO JUMPED INTO THE RING BEFORE THE ALI – SPINKS FIGHT AND TOOK OFF HER CLOTHES IN FRONT OF 70,000 PEOPLE IN THE SUPERDOME"
"THEY WERE CAUGHT COMPLETELY BY SURPRISE," EDY WILLIAMS SAID, "IT WAS REALLY SCARY. THE WORST PART WAS RIGHT BEFORE I DID IT. I WAS STANDING RINGSIDE AND I WAS SCARED. BUT IT WAS THE MOST UNBELIEVABLE SENSATION, WHEN I WAS IN THE RING AND THEY WERE ALL CHEERING. I KNEW WHAT ALI MUST FEEL LIKE."
EDY WILLIAMS "THE LAST STARLET" 5/27/1981

"BLOOD, SWEAT AND CHEERS"

"A WOMAN IN A BRIGHT RED GOWN INSINUATED HERSELF INTO THE CENTER OF THE RING OUT OF THIN AIR; IT WASN'T UNTIL SHE DOFFED THE HALTER TOP THAT ANY SERIOUS CHEERING BEGAN."
"BLOOD, SWEAT AND CHEERS"
SPORTS ILLUSTRATED — SEPTEMBER 25, 1978

EDY WILLIAMS

"THE LAST STARLET"

"EDY'S CLOTHES WERE DOWN"

"BUT WHEN THE CHIPS AND MOST OF EDY'S CLOTHES WERE DOWN,
ABC WAS TAKING A STATION BREAK."
"BLOOD, SWEAT AND CHEERS"
SPORTS ILLUSTRATED – 9/25/78

"EVERLASTING"

"SHE WAS APPREHENDED WEARING ONLY A G-STRING BY A MUSCULAR GUY FROM SECURITY. TO IT'S EVERLASTING CREDIT, THE CROWD BOOED LUSTILY AT THE DECIDEDLY HIGH HANDED MANNER IN WHICH THE LADY WAS REMOVED FROM THE PREMISES."
"BLOOD, SWEAT AND CHEERS"

"THE BUTTERFLY AND ME"

"THE BUTTERFLY AND ME HAVE BEEN THROUGH SOME UPS AND DOWNS AND THERE HAS BEEN LOTS OF EMOTION, MANY OF THEM BAD. BUT I HAVE FORGIVEN HIM. I HAD TO. YOU CANNOT HOLD OUT FOREVER. THERE WERE BRUISES IN MY HEART BECAUSE OF THE WORDS HE USED. I SPENT YEARS DREAMING ABOUT IT AND WANTING TO HURT HIM."

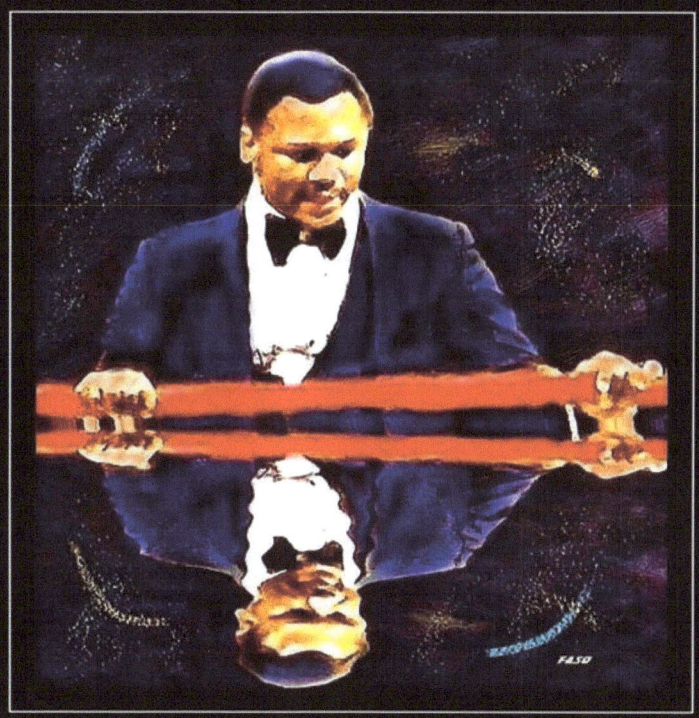

"BUT YOU HAVE TO THROW THAT STICK OUT OF THE WINDOW. DON'T FORGET THAT WE NEEDED EACH OTHER TO PRODUCE SOME OF THE GREATEST FIGHTS OF ALL TIME."

JOE FRAZIER – HEAVYWEIGHT CHAMPION

"THE BEST IN ME"

"I ALWAYS BRING OUT THE BEST IN MEN, BUT JOE FRAZIER, I WILL TELL THE WORLD RIGHT NOW, BRINGS OUT THE BEST IN ME. I'M GONNA TELL YA, THAT'S ONE HELLUVA MAN, AND GOD BLESS HIM."
MUHAMMAD ALI – AFTER- "THRILLER IN MANILA"

"AND NOW THE STRUGGLE GROWS GREATER TO GET TO THE RING....
THE WALK SEEMS ALMOST INTERMINABLE"

HOWARD COSELL – ABC SPORTS

"ALI TRANSFORMED A BOXING MATCH INTO AN EVENT"

FASO

"ALI TRANSFORMED A BOXING MATCH INTO AN EVENT BY MAKING IT MORE THAN JUST TWO OPPONENTS VYING FOR A WIN. WHEN ALI WAS INVOLVED, HE SEEMED TO ALWAYS MAKE THE EVENT LARGER THAN LIFE. THE EXCITEMENT OF WATCHING ONE OF HIS BOUTS DID NOT SOLELY INVOLVE THE OUTCOME. WOULD ALI KNOCK HIS OPPONENT DOWN IN THE ROUND THAT HE PREDICTED? IS HE PLAYING HURT? THERE WERE A MYRIAD OF QUESTIONS AND THOUGHTS THAT KEPT THE SPECTATOR'S INTEREST. HIS BOUTS WERE ALMOST ALWAYS A CENTRAL TOPIC OF DISCUSSION IN AMERICA."

JOHN C. MERINGOLO – FOUNDER – PUBLISHER – SILVER STAR MEDIA GROUP, INC.

"FINGERS ARE SORE"

"I'VE RECEIVED MORE PUBLICITY THAN ANY FIGHTER IN HISTORY.
I TALK TO REPORTERS UNTIL THEIR FINGERS ARE SORE."
-MUHAMMAD ALI-

"CONCEPT OF A LIVING LEGEND"

"MUHAMMAD ALI IS THE EPITOME OF THE CONCEPT OF A LIVING LEGEND. HE HAS INSPIRED AND THRILLED GENERATIONS OF FANS AROUND THE WORLD AS AN ATHLETE AND HUMAN BEING. THROUGHOUT HIS LIFE HE HAS BEEN ONE OF A KIND. THEY TRULY THREW AWAY THE MOLD WHEN HE WAS BORN."
KAREEM ABDUL-JABBAR- NBA ALL STAR

"THE UPROAR IS DEAFENING"

"ALI IS A GIANT. A POSITIVE LEGEND...AND NOW HE HAS MADE IT TO THE RING!
LISTEN!
25 YEARS OF SPORTS AND I HAVE NEVER HEARD A CROWD LIKE THIS!"
HOWARD COSELL – ABC SPORTS

"HE DESERVES IT"

"IT'S HARMONY TO ME WHEN I HEAR PEOPLE SAY MUHAMMAD ALI IS THE GREATEST. WHEN THEY CALL HIM THE GREATEST AND HE WALKS AROUND AND PEOPLE GIVE HIM STANDING OVATIONS, AND I'M THINKING HE DESERVES IT."
GEORGE FOREMAN – FACING ALI BY STEPHEN BRUNT

"IT WAS AN HONOR"

"IT WAS AN HONOR FOR ME TO HAVE BEEN IN THE RING WITH ALI."
TUNNEY HUNSAKER – ALI'S FIRST PROFESSIONAL OPPONENT WHO LOST TO ALI ON OCTOBER 29, 1960
LAUNCHING THE VICTORIOUS MUHAMMAD ALI ON THE GREATEST PROFESSIONAL BOXING CAREER OF ALL TIMES.

"THE ONE"

"HE IS THE ONE THEY WANTED TO SEE.
HE IS THE STORYLINE FOR HIS WHOLE LIFE."
HOWARD COSELL- ABC SPORTS

"THE FACE IN A CROWD"

"THERE IS ALI, THE FACE IN A CROWD, HE HAS BEEN SOMBER.
THERE HAS BEEN LITTLE OR NO CLOWNING.
HE HAS BEEN ALL PURPOSE FOR THIS."
HOWARD COSELL – ABC SPORTS

"SHOCK IN SEEING HIM"

"THERE WAS ALWAYS A SHOCK IN SEEING HIM AGAIN...THE WORLD'S GREATEST ATHLETE IS IN DANGER OF BEING OUR MOST BEAUTIFUL MAN, AND THE VOCABULARY OF CAMP IS BOUND TO APPEAR. WOMEN WOULD DRAW AN AUDIBLE BREATH, MEN WOULD LOOK DOWN."
"THE FIGHT" BY NORMAN MAILER

"RUMBLE YOUNG MAN- RUMBLE"

"WE GON' FLOAT LIKE A BUTTERFLY AND STING LIKE A BEE............."
AH!

"RUMBLE YOUNG MAN – RUMBLE"
BUNDINI BROWN – MUHAMMAD ALI RINGMAN

"THE CONFUSED CHAMPION"

"SPINKS HAD ARRIVED AT THE RING WITH AN ENTOURAGE OF 11, INCLUDING A TEAM OF MARINE CORP BUDDIES AND ALL THAT UNCOORDINATED LOT TOOK A HAND IN SHOUTING INSTRUCTION TO THE CONFUSED CHAMPION."
PAT PUTNAM – BOXING WRITER SPORTS ILLUSTRATED

"THE FIRST PUNCH"

"MUHAMMAD ALI COULD BEAT PEOPLE BEFORE THE MATCH EVEN STARTED.
HE COULD WIN BEFORE THE FIRST PUNCH WAS THROWN.
NOT TOO MANY PEOPLE CAN DO THAT."
TONY STEWART – INDY AND NASCAR CHAMPION

"ONE OF THE GREATEST MEN I EVER MET"

"WHAT MAKES MUHAMMAD ALI SPECIAL IS THAT HE LOVES LIFE. HE DIDN'T FALL IN LOVE WITH BEING YOUNG AND DOING THE SHUFFLE, HE FELL IN LOVE WITH LIFE. I DO BELIEVE HE'S "THE GREATEST", BUT FORGET ABOUT BOXING. GIVE THAT TO JOE LOUIS OR SOMEBODY. I BELIEVE HE'S ONE OF THE GREATEST MEN I EVER MET."
GEORGE FOREMAN – HEAVYWEIGHT CHAMPION

"I ONLY TALK WINNING"

FASO

"ANY FIGHTER DIDN'T LIKE MUHAMMAD ALI SHOULD HAVE HIS HEAD EXAMINED. BECAUSE ALI DID SO MUCH FOR BOXING."
ANGELO DUNDEE – ALI'S LIFELONG TRAINER

"IN BED BEFORE THE ROOM WAS DARK"

"I'M SO FAST THAT LAST NIGHT I TURNED OFF THE LIGHT SWITCH IN MY HOTEL ROOM AND WAS IN THE BED BEFORE THE ROOM WAS DARK!"
-MUHAMMAD ALI-

ON MUHAMMAD ALI

"EVEN PEOPLE WHO DIDN'T LIKE HIM, LIKED HIM."
ANGELO DUNDEE – MUHAMMAD ALI'S LIFETIME TRAINER

"HE STANDS TALL"

"THE MOST MEMORABLE THING ABOUT ALI IS THAT HE COULD NEVER BE COUNTED OUT. IT SEEMED IMPOSSIBLE TO BELIEVE HE HAD NOTHING LEFT, THAT APPLIED NOT ONLY TO HIS BOXING CAREER, BUT TO HIS LIFE. HE STILL STANDS TALL, SAYS WHAT HE BELIEVES AND ACCEPTS THE CONSEQUENCES OF HIS DECISIONS. HE IS THE DEFINITION OF AN AMERICAN, HE IS HONEST AND PRINCIPLED. HE IS THE GREATEST."

JOHN C. MERINGOLO – FOUNDER-PUBLISHER-SILVER STAR MEDIA GROUP, INC.

"A PIED PIPER"

FASO

"ALI WAS A GREAT ATHLETE AND A PIED PIPER WHO EVERYONE WANTED TO FOLLOW
HE WAS THE BIGGEST KID AND THE STRONGEST MAN. HE COULD DO MAGIC TRICKS-
HE HAS THAT TWINKLE IN HIS EYE – THAT PLAYFULNESS, BOMBAST AND POLITICS.
ALL OF WHICH WERE UNIQUE IN AN ATHLETE."
LARRY MERCHANT –HBO SPORTS COMMENTATOR & WRITER

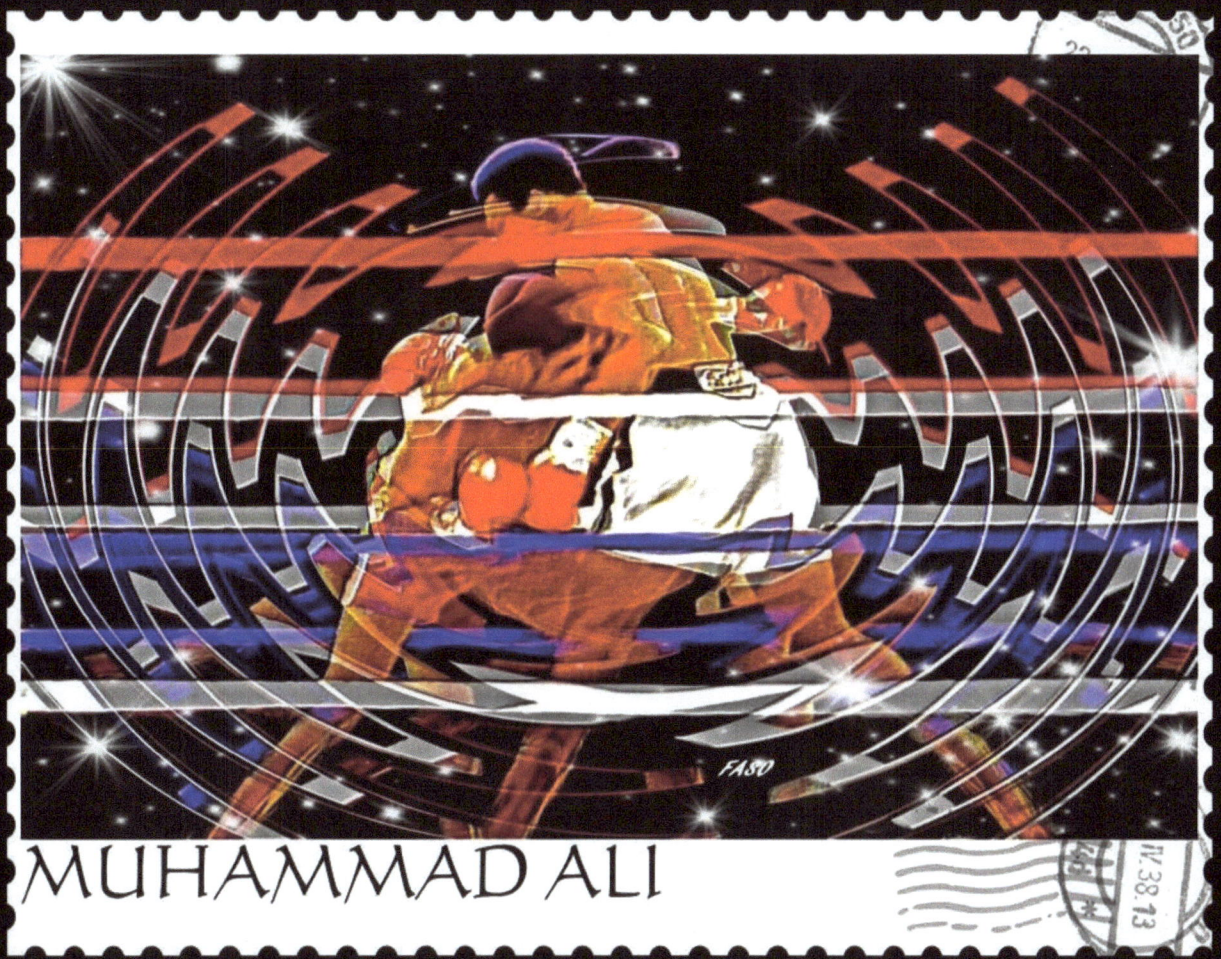

"FIFTEEN REFEREES"

FASO

"FIFTEEN REFEREES. I WANT 15 REFEREES TO BE AT THIS FIGHT BECAUSE THERE AIN'T NO ONE MAN WHO CAN KEEP UP WITH THE PACE I SET EXCEPT ME." -MUHAMMAD ALI-

"EXTREMELY TRUCULENT"

"ALI COULD REPRESENT EVERY KID WHO EVER FLOUTED AUTHORITY. THE FIGHTER FOREVER TITILLATED SPECTATORS WITH PANTOMIMED THREATS TO LIFT THE BROADCASTER'S HAIRPIECE AND ONCE SAID, "COSELL, YOU'RE A PHONY, AND THAT THING ON YOUR HEAD COMES FROM THE TAIL OF A PONY." TO A COSELL SCOLDING OF, "YOU'RE BEING EXTREMELY TRUCULENT." THE DEFIANT CHILD ALI REPLIED, "WHATEVER "TRUCULENT" MEANS IF THAT'S GOOD, I'M THAT."
DAVE KINDRED –AUTHOR- "SOUND AND FURY"

"THIS WOULD BE MY SHOW"

"THIS WOULD BE MY SHOW IF I HAD THE RIGHT COMPLEXION
TO GET THE PROTECTION."
MUHAMMAD ALI TO FRANK GIFFORD – PRE-FIGHT INTERVIEW

"I LOVE YOUR SHOW"

FASO

"I LOVE YOUR SHOW, I ADMIRE YOUR STYLE, BUT YOUR PAYMENTS ARE SO CHEAP, I WON'T SEE YOU FOR A WHILE."
MUHAMMAD ALI TO FRANK GIFFORD – PRE-FIGHT INTERVIEW

"ONE OF THE RARE, RARE CATS"

"TAKE THAT TRIP WITH MUHAMMAD ALI BECAUSE HE IS A TRIP ALTOGETHER.
YOU ARE A PIECE OF WORK...AND PRETTY TOO...
ONE OF THE RARE, RARE CATS."
FRANK GIFFORD – ABC SPORTS

"HE WAS A PARADOX"

FASO

"TO CUS D'AMATO, THE LATE QUINTESSENTIAL BOXING MANAGER, MUHAMMAD ALI WAS THE PERFECT BOXER, "HE WAS A PARADOX." CUS ONCE TOLD ME... "HIS PHYSICAL PERFORMANCES IN THE RING WERE ABSOLUTELY WRONG. BUT VERY MUCH ENTERTAINING. YET HIS BRAIN WAS ALWAYS IN PERFECT CONDITION. HE SHOWED US ALL" CUS CONTINUED WITH A BROAD SMILE WRITTEN ACROSS HIS FACE, "THAT VICTORY COMES FROM HERE," HITTING HIS FOREHEAD WITH HIS INDEX FINGER. THEN HE WAIVED A PAIR OF FISTS AND LOOKING AT THEM SAID; "NOT FROM HERE.:
JOSE TORRES —LIGHT HEAVYWEIGHT CHAMPION

"A BIG HEART"

"HE HAD A BIG HEART, GOOD CHIN, FAST FEET, FAST HANDS — WHAT MORE COULD YOU WANT.?"
-SIR HENRY COOPER-

"A HERO TO ME"

"ALI HAS ALWAYS BEEN A HERO TO ME. HERE IS A KID FROM LOUISVILLE WITHOUT AN EDUCATION, WHO WAS A FIGHTER AND CAPTIVATED THE WORLD – NO ONE WILL EVER BE LIKE ALI. THERE IS ONE AND ONLY ONE ALI. HE WILL GO DOWN AS ONE OF THE GREATEST HUMAN BEINGS TO WALK THE EARTH."
DANA WHITE – PRESIDENT – ULTIMATE FIGHTING CHAMPIONSHIP

"PIECE OF CEMENT"

"HITTING ALI IN THE BODY OR ON THE ARMS WAS LIKE HITTING A PIECE OF CEMENT."
KEN NORTON – HEAVYWEIGHT CHAMPION

"THE MAN IN THE GREY SWEAT SUIT"

"I WAS NINE YEARS OLD AND TRAINING IN EAST LOS ANGLES AT THE RESURRECTION BOXING GYM. MANY KIDS WOULD TRAIN, SKIPPING ROPE, HITTING THE HEAVY BAG.

ONE DAY A MAN – WEARING A SWEAT SUIT COMES IN. HE IS CARRYING A LITTLE TOTE BAG – HE STARTS HITTING THE HEAVY BAG...ALL OF A SUDDEN, HE CALLS A GROUP OF US OVER –

"I WANT TO TEACH YOU HOW TO HIT THE HEAVY BAG", HE SAYS. HE KEEPS SAYING...
"STAY ON YOUR TOES – STAY ON YOUR TOES."

IT SO HAPPENED THAT MAN WAS MUHAMMAD ALI.
WHAT STRUCK ME ABOUT HIM WAS THAT WHEN HE TAUGHT US, HE ALWAYS MADE US LAUGH. HE WENT OUT OF HIS WAY TO MAKE US LAUGH. HE WANTED US TO ENJOY OURSELVES.
TO ENJOY THE GAME OF BOXING.

MUHAMMAD ALI

I CAN STILL SEE HIM. THE MAN IN THE GREY SWEAT SUIT LIKE IT WAS YESTERDAY.
I HAVE STARTED TO REALIZE, HERE IS A MAN WHO REACHED GREAT SUCCESS IN THE RING.
THE GREATEST OF ALL TIME – AN ICON, BUT HE WALKED INTO THAT GYM ALONE AS SOMEONE WHO FAILED AT EVERYTHING. IT HAS CROSSED MY MIND LATELY – MAYBE I SHOULD SHOW UP AT A GYM ONE DAY, JUST TO MAKE A KID FEEL LIKE MUHAMMAD ALI MADE ME FEEL."
OSCAR DELA HOYA
OLYMPIC GOLD WORLD TITLES IN SIX BOXING DIVISIONS

"AN AMERICAN TREASURE"

"MUHAMMAD ALI IS ONE OF THE FEW PEOPLE WHO CAN REALLY SAY THEY ARE "THE GREATEST" IN THE WORLD...AND REALLY BACK IT UP. HE TRANSCENDS TIME, REMAINS RELENTING TO THE PEOPLE OF ALL AGES AND TRULY IS AN AMERICAN TREASURE. OUR CAREERS PLAYED OUT TOGETHER, AND OFTEN WE SPENT TIME TOGETHER SIDE BY SIDE AT AWARDS BANQUETS AND TO THIS DAY, EVERY TIME OUR PATHS CROSS, HE LEANS CLOSE TO ME AND SAYS, "BILLIE JEAN, YOU'RE THE QUEEN." YES, MUHAMMAD ALI, YOU TRULY ARE "THE GREATEST" ...AND YOU ARE THE KING."

BILLIE JEAN KING - TENNIS STAR

"THE COMPLETE PACKAGE"

"AS A FIGHTER, ALI WAS THE COMPLETE PACKAGE, A RING STRATEGIST, HIS TIMING, FOOTWORK SPEED AND HOW HE PLAYED THE MENTAL GAME AND PROMOTED HIS FIGHTS. I WOULD HAVE LOVED TO HAVE SEEN HIM IN PERSON...HE WAS JUST THE BEST."
CHUCK "THE ICEMAN" LIDDELL – ULTIMATE FIGHTING CHAMPION

"WELL, I'M STILL PRETTY"

"WELL, I'M STILL PRETTY AND HE'S IN THE HOSPITAL. I'LL FIGHT ANYBODY THE PUBLIC WANTS ME TO FIGHT NOW."
-MUHAMMAD ALI- AFTER WINNING HIS FIRST TITLE FIGHT

"A MAGNIFICENT FIGHTER"

"MUHAMMAD ALI — HE WAS A MAGNIFICENT FIGHTER AND HE WAS AN ICON — THE GREATEST OF ALL TIME."
DON KING — BOXING PROMOTER

"THE GREATEST AMERICAN"

FASO

"CHAMP.... YOU ARE THE GREATEST AMERICAN OF OUR GENERATION."
DANNY LYON – PHOTOGRAPHER – MAGNUM

"ONE OF THE GREATEST FIGHTERS OF ALL TIMES"

"MUHAMMAD COULD TAKE A VERY GOOD PUNCH. HE WAS SLICK, HE COULD MOVE, MAKE YOU MISS, GOOD HAND SPEED AND COMBINATIONS AND ONE OF THE GREATEST FIGHTERS OF ALL TIME IN MY OPINION."
LARRY HOLMES – HEAVYWEIGHT CHAMPION

"GREATEST MOVING HEAVYWEIGHT"

"BUT YOU HAVE TO ADMIRE MUHAMMAD, HE WILL GO DOWN IN HISTORY AS THE GREATEST MOVING HEAVYWEIGHT OF ALL TIME." SIR HENRY COOPER – FROM MUHAMMAD ALI: "THROUGH THE EYES OF THE WORLD" BY MARK COLLINS

"HE PERFORMED HEROICALLY"

"I PARTICULARLY ADMIRE PEOPLE WHO MAKE A CONTRIBUTION, WHO TAKE THEIR KNOCKS AND COME BACK, AND ALI HANDLED HIMSELF DAMN WELL UNDER CIRCUMSTANCES THAT WERE INFINITELY MORE DIFFICULT THAN ANY I EVER FACED.
HE PERFORMED HEROICALLY IN AND OUT OF THE RING."
JAMES MICHENER, PULITZER PRIZE AUTHOR IN "MUHAMMAD ALI; HIS LIFE AND TIMES"
BY T. HOUSER

HEAVYWEIGHT CHAMPION
LEON SPINKS

LEON SPINKS FOUGHT MUHAMMAD ALI AS THE CURRENT HEAVYWEIGHT CHAMPION AND WAS THE ONLY MAN EVER TO TAKE THE TITLE FROM ALI IN THE RING. MUHAMMAD ALI'S OTHER LOSSES WERE NON TITLE CONTESTS OR BOUTS WHERE ALI WAS THE CHALLENGER. SPINKS HELD THE TITLE FROM 2/15/78 - 9/15/79 WHEN ALI WON THE 3RD TITLE.

"IN SEARCH OF ALI"

"SPINKS WENT OUT IN SEARCH OF ALI, HE FOUND FRED ASTAIRE. ALI TURNED THEIR FISTFIGHT INTO A SERIES OF THREE MINUTE DANCE RECITALS. AFTER EACH EMBRACE, ALI WAITED FOR THE REFEREE'S BREAK AND THEN DANCED AWAY, WALTZING SOMETIMES TO THE LEFT, QUICK-STEPPING SOMETIMES TO THE RIGHT. ALWAYS OUT OF HARM'S WAY." PAT PUTNAM – BOXING WRITER – SPORTS ILLUSTRATED

"THEN DANCED AWAY"

"WALTZING SOMETIMES TO THE LEFT, QUICKSTEPPING TO THE RIGHT."
-PAT PUTNAM-

"THE MASTER ARTIST"

"REFEREE, LUCIAN JOUBERT INDICATED HE WOULD PREFER SOMETHING A LITTLE MORE PURE FROM THE MASTER ARTIST, AND HE EXPRESSED HIS DISPLEASURE BY WARNING ALI IN THE EARLY ROUNDS FOR GRABBING FROM BEHIND THE HEAD."
PAT PUTNAM – BOXING WRITER – SPORTS ILLUSTRATED

ALI HAS ONE ROUND TAKEN

"AFTER FIVE ROUNDS OF GRABBING SPINKS BEHIND THE HEAD, REFEREE JOUBERT TOLD DUNDEE THAT HE WAS TAKING A ROUND AWAY FROM ALI, "WHAT THE HELL FOR?" SCREAMED DUNDEE, "YOU TAKE A ROUND AWAY FROM A GUY FOR HOLDING AND YOU JUST NOW TELL ME ABOUT IT? WHAT THE HELL WERE YOU WAITING FOR?"
PAT PUTNAM

"WHERE DID HE GO, LEON?"

"FROM THE FIFTH ROUND ON, DUNDEE BEGAN SHOUTING ACROSS THE RING AT THE FRUSTRATED CHAMPION: WHERE DID HE GO LEON? WHERE DID HE GO?"
PAT PUTNAM – BOXING WRITER – SPORTS ILLUSTRATED

"POETICALLY SIMPLE"

'ALI'S STRATEGY WAS POETICALLY SIMPLE: JAB, JAB, THROW A RIGHT AND GRAB. WHEN SPINKS CAME IN FLAILING, AS IS HIS BENT, ALI SIMPLY HOOKED HIS LEFT HAND AROUND THE BACK OF THE YOUNG INCUMBENT'S HEAD AND PULLED HIM INTO AN EMBRACE, QUITE EFFECTIVELY LIMITING HIM TO ONE OR TWO DEFUSED PUNCHES, AND PULLING HIM OFF BALANCE."
PAT PUTNAM – BOXING WRITER – SPORTS ILLUSTRATED

"AND WHEN IN DOUBT"

FASO

"AND WHEN IN DOUBT, ALI SIMPLY DREW SPINKS TO HIM IN A MIGHTY BEAR HUG, WHERE, AT 221 POUNDS TO 201, IT WAS NO CONTEST."
PAT PUTNAM – BOXING WRITER – SPORTS ILLUSTRATED

"GOODBYE LEON"

FASO

"NOW, INSTEAD OF JUST THROWING ONE PUNCH AFTER A JAB, ALI BEGAN TRIGGERING COMBINATIONS. WHICH IF NOT PAINFUL, WERE IMMENSELY POINT PRODUCTIVE. "GOODBYE LEON: SHOUTED DUNDEE AS ONE THREE – PUNCH COMBINATION ASSAULTED THE FORMER MARINE."
PAT PUTNAM – BOXING WRITER – SPORTS ILLUSTRATED

"TRY TO HIT ALI"

FASO

"DON'T GET HIT! MOVE IN! RUN! CIRCLE TO YOUR RIGHT! TRY TO HIT ALI!
MOVE TO YOUR LEFT! BACK UP! ATTACK! WHEN HE JABS, DUCK. WHEN HE JABS, YOU JAB WHEN
HE JABS, JUMP UP AND CLICK YOUR HEELS THREE TIMES AND WHISTLE —
SHAVE AND A HAIRCUT, TWO BITS!"
SPINK'S CORNER AS RELATED BY PAT PUTMAN

"KNOCK IT OFF"

"STUNG BUT UNHURT, SPINKS TURNED AND GRINNED AT ALI'S LITTLE TRAINER. AT THE END OF THE SEVENTH ROUND, WITH SPINKS UNABLE TO MOUNT ANY KIND OF RECOGNIZABLE OFFENSE, ALI PERMITTED HIMSELF JUST ONE LITTLE, "ALI SHUFFLE" ON THE WAY BACK TO HIS CORNER. "KNOCK IT OFF" GROWLED DUNDEE AFTER ALI HAD SAT DOWN."

PAT PUTNAM -BOXING WRITER – SPORTS ILLUSTRATED

"THE ENSUING BABBLE"

"FROM THE OTHER CORNER, DUNDEE WATCHED THE ENSUING BABBLE, THEN TURNED AND STUDIED THE USUAL TWO DOZEN OR SO MEMBERS OF ALI'S TEAM. "WELL" HE SAID, "THEIR CRAZIES CAN CERTAINLY MATCH OUR CRAZIES."
PAT PUTNAM – WRITER- SPORTS ILLUSTRATED

"THE DETERMINED FOE"

"NOW FACED WITH THE DETERMINED FOE HE HAD EXPECTED TO FIGHT LAST FEBRUARY. THE BAFFLED SPINKS KEPT LOOKING TO HIS CORNER FOR ADVICE. WHAT HE FOUND WAS CHAOS. HE WOULD HAVE BEEN BETTER SERVED TO ASK THE RING POST FOR COUNSEL."
PAT PUTNAM — WRITER — SPORTS ILLUSTRATED

"CONFUSION CORNER"

"FOR THE 25-YEAR-OLD SPINKS, THE SITUATION WAS THE SAME, ONLY MORE DESPERATE. IT CHANGED TO FATAL WHEN GEORGE BENTON, THE BRILLIANT TRAINER WHO MASTERMINDED THE STUNNING UPSET OF ALI IN LAS VEGAS STORMED OUT OF THE CORNER AFTER THE 7TH ROUND AND THE ARENA AFTER 12TH. "BY GOD IT'S A DAMN ZOO IN THERE" SAID BENTON AS HE LEFT SPINKS.
PAT PUTNAM

INSIDE MUHAMMAD ALI

"EVERY TIME AN OPPONENT OF ALI'S WALKED INTO THE RING ENRAGED OR INTIMIDATED, "THE GREATEST" HAD DONE HIS JOB. HE'D ALREADY, MAGICALLY, CLOGGED HIS RIVAL'S "RADAR". AFFECTING IN THE PROCESS HIS ABILITY TO SEE EVERY COMING PUNCH. A HYSTERICAL OR SCARED FIGHTER COULD NEVER ENGAGE THE SEEMINGLY EXCITED BUT TOTALLY RELAXED ALI IN A RING WITH ANY EXPECTATION OF SUCCESS. "THE GREATEST" SIMPLY INVITED THOSE TRULY INTERESTED ON "THE ART OF SELF DEFENSE" TO WATCH NOT THE BULLET, MISSILE, OR BOMB THAT EVERYONE SAW STRIKE THE OPPOSITION, BUT TO UNDERSTAND THE UNSEEN DEVICES THAT PREPARED AND PROPELLED THE AMMUNITION TO THE BULL'S EYE MORE OFTEN THAN NOT.

THESE CLANDESTINE TRIGGERS ARE BETTER KNOWN AS CHARACTER (WILL, DESIRE, DETERMINATION) AND INTELLIGENCE (TIMING AND ACCURACY). WHEN A BOXER HAS THESE PSYCHOLOGICAL AND EMOTIONAL ELEMENTS IN WORKING ORDER. HIS/HER PUNCHES BECOME FAULTLESS MISSILES OF VICTORY. HE/SHE IS READY TO JOIN A CHAMPS REIGN IN ANY BATTLEFIELD. SUCH EFFERVESCENCE IS CLEARLY CONVEYED TO US ALL BY EVERY CHAMPION BUT NONE HAVE DONE IT MORE PROMINENTLY AND DELIBERATELY THAN THE ARTISTIC GENIUS OF MUHAMMAD ALI. LAMENTABLY, ONLY A FEW HAVE BOTHERED TO SEARCH SERIOUSLY THROUGHOUT THE HIDDEN ARSENAL OF EVERY BOXING CHAMPION. ALI WENT AS FAR AS TO LIMIT HIS PHYSICAL WEAPONRY IN ORDER TO STRENGTHEN AND HIGHLIGHT HIS PSYCHOLOGICAL AND EMOTIONAL ONES. NO ONE EVER SAW HIM PUNCHING BELOW THE JAW, OR WITNESSED ALI BLOCKING PUNCHES WITH HIS ARMS AND ELBOWS LIKE EVERY OTHER GOOD CHAMPION. HE PUNCHED IN RALLIES LIKE AN AMATEUR RATHER THAN IN SETS OF COMBINATIONS LIKE EVERY OTHER GOOD CHAMPION. HE DIDN'T SLIP PUNCHES OR BEND UNDER THEM. INSTEAD, HE PULLED HIS TORSO BACK TO EVADE THE IMPACT, LIKE SOMEONE IN THE MIDDLE OF A TRAIN TRACK TRYING TO AVOID BEING HIT BY AN INCOMING TRAIN NOT BY MOVING TO ONE OR THE OTHER SIDE OF THE TRACK, BUT BY RUNNING BACKWARDS.

ALI ALSO CARRIED HIS GUARD LOW, HIS JAW FOREVER EXPOSED. A DEFINITE NO – NO IN BOXING NO BOXER CAN EVER GET AWAY WITH SUCH HORRIFIC FAULTS, EXCEPT THAT IS, OF COURSE, MUHAMMAD ALI. IN FACT, DOZENS OF HIS IMITATORS – SOME WITH GREAT TALENT – WOUND UP WITH SHORT, AWFUL CAREERS NEVER KNOWING THAT THEY ALL LACKED ALI'S EMOTIONAL AND PSYCHOLOGICAL SUPREMACY IN THE RING."

"ON MUHAMMAD ALI" BY JOSE TORRES
HEAVYWEIGHT CHAMPION – AUTHOR OF "STING LIKE A BEE"

"EVERYTHING CHANGES"

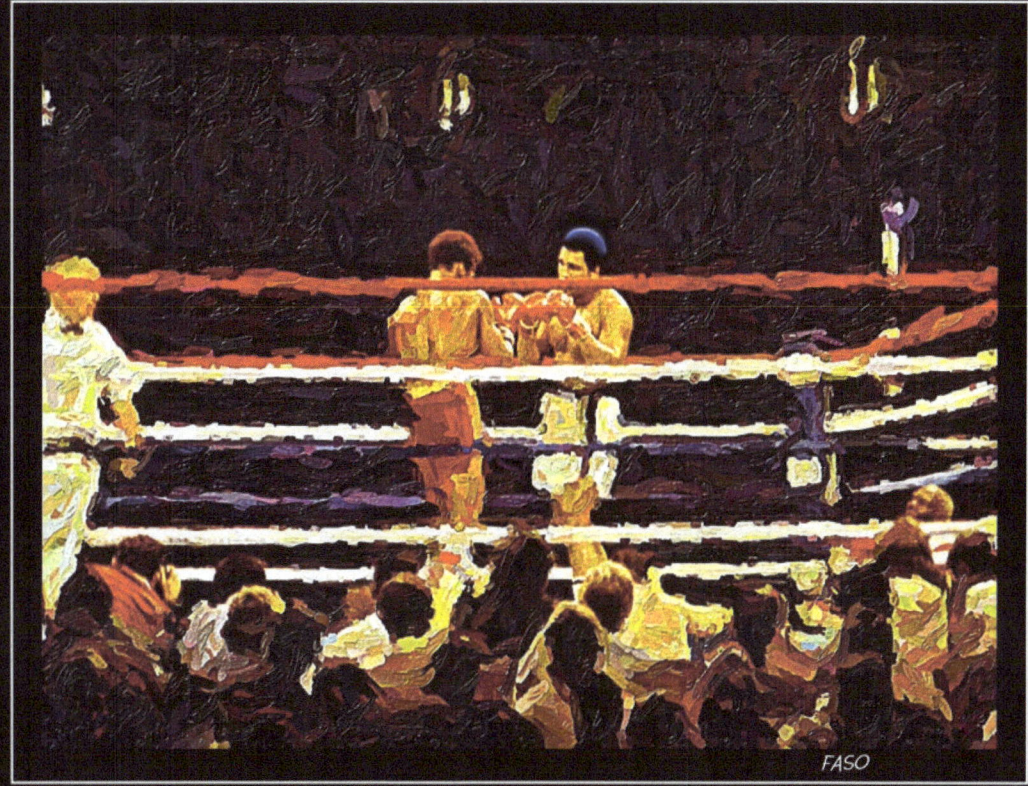

"NOTHING IS THE SAME ANYMORE, NOT EVEN THE KING OF THE WORLD HIMSELF. THE ONLY CHAMPION WHOSE TITLE SEEMED TO HAVE A QUALITY OF THE UNIVERSAL, OR AS BUNDINI BROWN CALLS HIM: THE BLESSING OF THE PLANET. "EVERYTHING CHANGES" SAYS MUHAMMAD ALI. "GOVERNMENTS CHANGE, KINGS FALL, PEOPLE CHANGE. I'VE CHANGED."
"HE MOVES LIKE SILK, HITS LIKE A TON" BY MARK KRAM, SPORTS ILLUSTRATED OCT. 26, 1970

"BIGGER THAN BOXING"

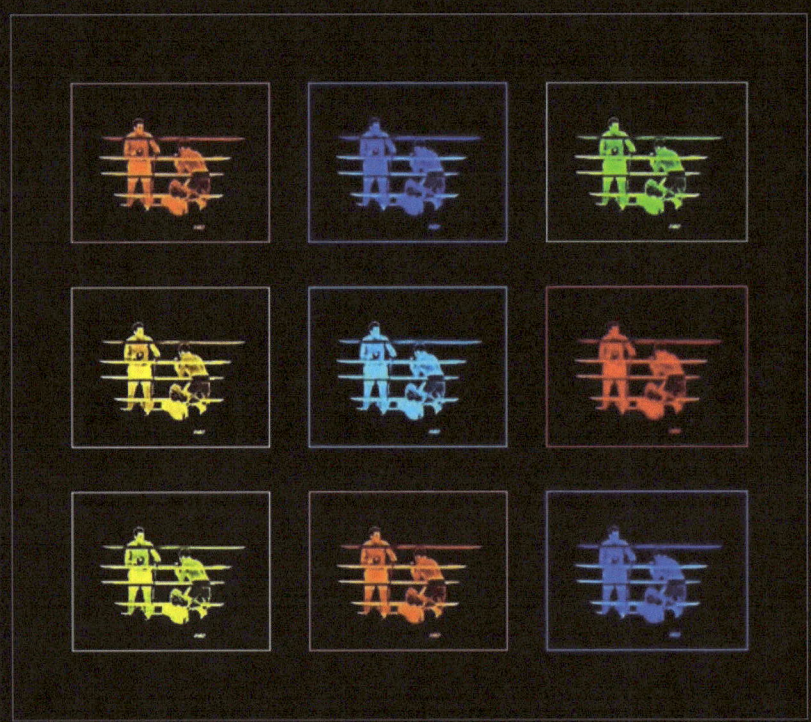

"MY FATHER LOVED ALI. HE WAS THE ONE THAT INTRODUCED ME TO BOXING AND MUHAMMAD ALI. EVER SINCE ALI HAS BEEN – ONE OF MY GREATEST INSPIRATIONS. THE GREATEST WILL ALWAYS BE THE GREATEST. TO ME ALI IS MORE THAT BOXING...HE IS A LIFE TEACHER, BIGGER THAN BOXING ITSELF."
ZIGGY MARLEY – SON OF BOB MARLEY

"WE COULD SEE HIS GREATNESS"

"WE COULD SEE HIS GREATNESS IN HIM WHEN HE AS 12. HE WAS GREAT. HE WAS HAPPY, JOLLY, GAY, BEAUTIFUL, KIND, SWEET PERSON. HE WAS LOVING TO EVERYONE, BLACK OR WHITE. HE TAUGHT ME TO LOVE ALL KINDS OF PEOPLE. HE PROTECTED ME. HE WAS GENTLE...A BIG SWEETHEART, AS SMALL CHILDREN WE PREDICTED WE'D ONE DAY BE HERE. WE ARE JUST GRATEFUL TO GOD."
RAHAMAN ALI – MUHAMMAD ALI'S BROTHER

"THE GREATEST INVENTOR"

"MUHAMMAD ALI WAS ONE OF THE GREATEST INVENTORS OF ALL TIME. HE INVENTED A NEW WAY TO BOX. HE INVENTED A NEW WAY FOR ATHLETES AND CELEBRITIES TO TALK ABOUT THEMSELVES AND HE ESPECIALLY INVENTED THE MODERN WAY FOR PUBLIC FIGURES TO HAVE A SOCIAL CAUSE FOR WHICH THEY MADE A TRUE SACRIFICE. SO MUCH OF THE WORLD WE LIVE IN WAS PIONEERED BY MUHAMMAD ALI."
RICHARD STENGEL — MANAGING EDITOR — TIME MAGAZINE

MUHAMMAD ALI

"THE GREATEST OF ALL TIME"

"LARGER THAN LIFE"

"I WAS JUST A KID WHEN ALI FOUGHT SOME OF HIS GREATEST FIGHTS AGAINST JOE FRAZIER AND GEORGE FOREMAN, AND I REMEMBER THINKING THAT HE WAS JUST LARGER THAN LIFE AND HAD SUCH INCREDIBLE STYLE. I MIGHT NOT HAVE KNOWN THE WORDS "GLOBAL ICON" BACK THEN, BUT THAT HE WAS AND WILL BE FOR ALL TIME."
MICHAEL JORDAN – SIX TIME NBA CHAMPION

"I'M A FIGHTER"

"I'M A FIGHTER. I BELIEVE IN THE EYE-FOR-AN-EYE BUSINESS. I'M NO CHEEK TURNER. I GOT NO RESPECT FOR A MAN WHO WON'T HIT BACK. YOU KILL MY DOG. YOU BETTER HIDE YOUR CAT."
MUHAMMAD ALI

"EVERYTHING HE KNEW"

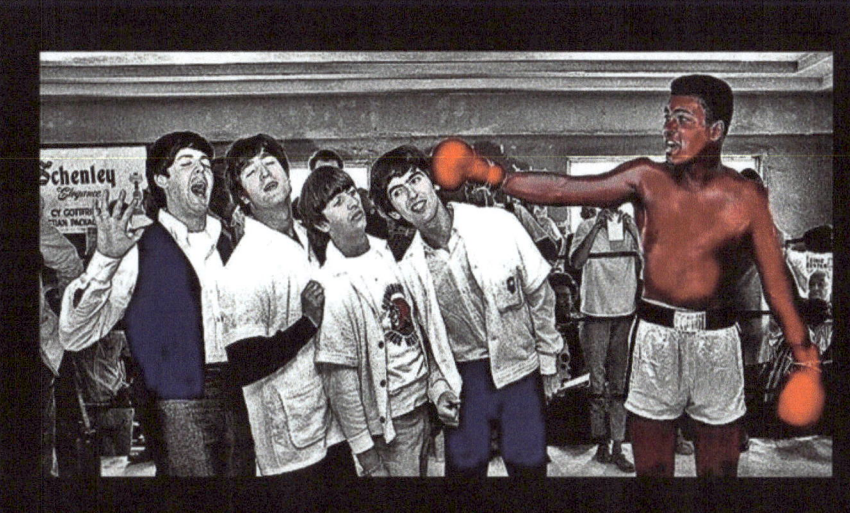

"I SPARRED WITH CASSIUS CLAY AS HE WAS KNOWN THEN.
I TAUGHT HIM EVERYTHING HE KNEW. THAT WAS A THRILL."
RINGO STARR – BEATLES – FROM "ANTHOLOGY"

"THE FIGHT DOCTOR"

"WHAT WAS IT LIKE TO BE MUHAMMAD ALI'S FIGHT DOCTOR?"
HE SAID:
"IT WAS LIKE BEING QUEEN VICTORIA'S GYNECOLOGIST —
THE TITLE DIDN'T MEAN MUCH, BUT THE VIEW WAS SPECTACULAR."
FERDIE PACHECHO = MUHAMMAD ALI'S "FIGHT DOCTOR"

"NEVER CONSIDER A FIGHTER A SON"

"I HAD MORE FUN WITH ALI THAN ANYONE IN MY LIFE...NO I DON'T CONSIDER HIM A SON. A TRAINER CAN'T EVER BE A FIGHTER'S FATHER. NEVER CONSIDER A FIGHTER A SON... YOU CAN'T HELP HIM. YOU CAN'T TAKE CARE OF YOUR OWN CHILD IF THEY HAVE A CUT, OR YOUR HAND STARTS SHAKING. HE IS MY FRIEND, ALI HAS SO MANY QUALITIES AS A HUMAN BEING. BACK THEN I HAD HIM TO THE HOUSE THREE CHRISTMASES. HE ENTERTAINED EVERYONE. HE WAS THE FIRST TO ARRIVE AND THE LAST TO LEAVE. ONE OF THE GREATEST THINGS THAT HAPPENED TO THE HUMAN RACE...HAVING ALI AROUND.
-ANGELO DUNDEE-

"THIS IS SERIOUS BUSINESS"

"NOBODY HAS TO TELL ME THIS IS SERIOUS BUSINESS, I AM NOT FIGHTING ONE MAN. I AM FIGHTING A LOT OF MEN. SHOWING A LOT OF 'EM...HERE IS ONE MAN THEY COULDN'T DEFEAT. COULDN'T CONQUERER. MY MISSION IS TO BRING FREEDOM TO 30 MILLION BLACK PEOPLE."
-MUHAMMAD ALI-

"INSIDE THE RING"

"INSIDE THE RING OR OUT, AIN'T NOTHING WRONG WITH GOING DOWN.
IT'S STAYING DOWN THAT'S WRONG."
-MUHAMMAD ALI-

"EVERY HEAD MUST BOW"

"I'M VAIN, I KNOW I'M GREAT, BUT WHEN IT COMES TO MUHAMMAD ALI, EVERY HEAD MUST BOW. THIS MAN IS THE GREATEST OF ALL TIME."
MIKE TYSON- HEAVYWEIGHT CHAMPION

"BACK IT UP"

"ITS NOT BRAGGING IF YOU CAN BACK IT UP."
-MUHAMMAD ALI-

"EXTRA LIFE INSURANCE"

"I'VE GOT SPEED, POWER AND ENDURANCE AND ANYONE
WHO FIGHTS ME HAD BETTER TAKE OUT EXTRA LIFE INSURANCE."
MUHAMMAD ALI

"DANCE UNDER THOSE LIGHTS"

"THE FIGHT IS WON OR LOST FAR AWAY FROM WITNESSES — BEHIND THE LINES, IN THE GYM, AND OUT THERE ON THE ROAD, LONG BEFORE I DANCE UNDER THOSE LIGHTS."
-MUHAMMAD ALI-

"LIGHT THE TORCH"

"I REMEMBER SEEING MUHAMMAD ALI LIGHT THE TORCH AT THE OLYMPIC GAMES IN 1996. HE WAS HOLDING THE TORCH. IT WAS LIKE HE WAS SAYING...I'M STILL PRETTY, ITS NEVER BEEN ABOUT MY FOOTWORK OR POEMS... IT WAS ABOUT ME. IT WAS AT THAT MOMENT THAT I REMEMBERED ALI REALLY WAS THE GREATEST."
GEORGE FOREMAN- HEAVYWEIGHT CHAMPION

"THE GREATEST OF ALL TIME"

"HE DECLARED HIMSELF "THE GREATEST" ... HE DIDN'T SAY THE GREATEST BOXER, ATHLETE OR HORSE'S ASS FOR THAT MATTER. HE DIDN'T CARE. HE SUPPLIED THE ADJECTIVE; SELECTING THE NOUN WAS YOUR BUSINESS. HE JUST SAID, "THE GREATEST OF ALL TIME" – I AGREE."
MICHAEL J FOX – ACTOR

"FLOAT LIKE A BUTTERFLY"

"FLOAT LIKE A BUTTERFLY, STING LIKE A BEE.
THE HANDS CAN'T HIT WHAT THE EYES CAN'T SEE."
-MUHAMMAD ALI-

"SEEN THE LIGHT"

"A ROOSTER CROWS ONLY WHEN IT SEES THE LIGHT,
PUT HIM IN THE DARK AND HE'LL NEVER CROW.
I HAVE SEEN THE LIGHT AND I'M CROWING."
-MUHAMMAD ALI-

"BELIEVE YOU ARE THE BEST"

"TO BE A GREAT CHAMPION, YOU MUST BELIEVE YOU ARE THE BEST.
IF YOU ARE NOT, PRETEND YOU ARE."
-MUHAMMAD ALI-

THE FINAL ROUND OF THE FINAL VICTORY

"I GOT HIT A LOT, I'M GLAD I LIVED THROUGH IT."
-LEON SPINKS- HEAVYWEIGHT CHAMPION-

"METHODICAL"

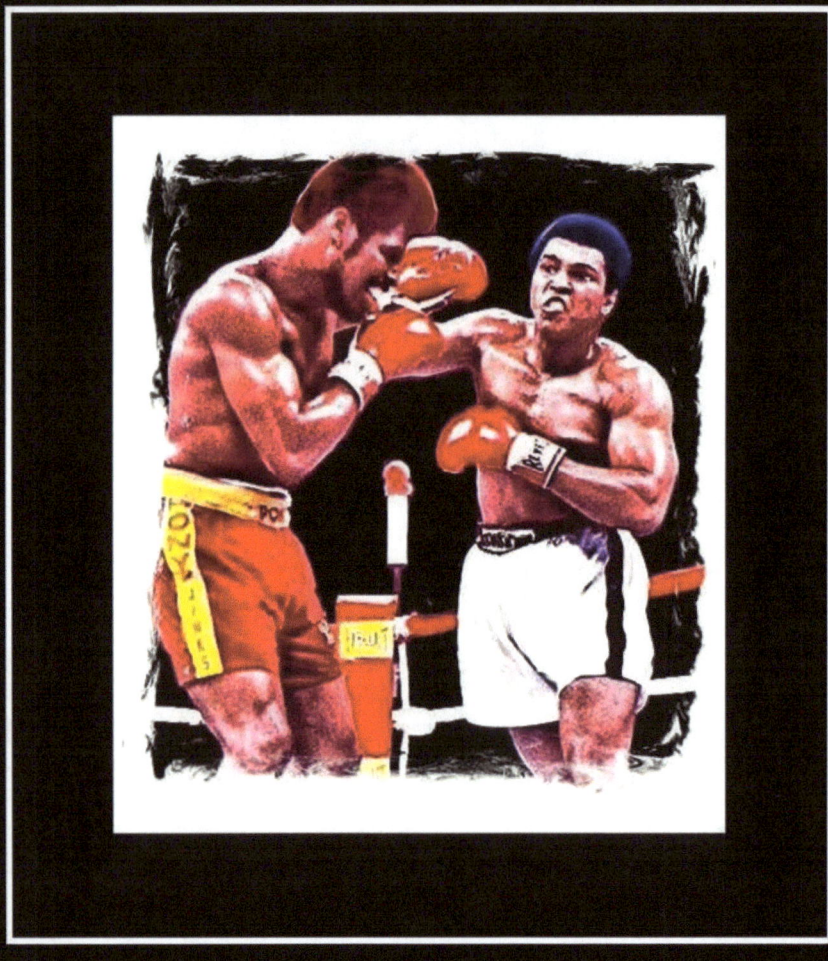

"THERE WERE NO STUNNING KNOCKDOWNS OR OVERWHELMING ROUNDS, BUT RATHER A METHODICAL BOXING EXHIBITION PUT ON BY A MASTER, A SOLID OFFENCE THAT TOOK BACK FROM LEON SPINKS THE CHAMPION'S CROWN THAT NEVER SEEMED TO FIT HIM PROPERLY."
-THE FINAL VICTORY-

"CLEAR VOICE OF DUNDEE"

"ALI CAN SURVIVE IN SUCH BEDLAM, FOR AWAYS, RISING ABOVE THE NONSENSE, IS THE CLEAR VOICE OF DUNDEE. IT IS ALI'S LIFE RAFT IN A SEA OF BATTLE HYSTERIA."
PAT PUTNAM – BOXING WRITER – SPORTS ILLUSTRATED

THE FINAL VICTORY

"THE 15 ROUND FIGHT WAS DIFFICULT FOR ALI AT 36 YEARS OF AGE AND WAS TELLING AFTER THE FINAL BELL. WHEN THE FIRST TO CLIMB INTO THE RING WAS HIS LIFELONG TRAINER, ANGELO DUNDEE. THIS WAS THE LAST PUBLIC MOMENT OF VICTORY FOR THE LEGENDARY CHAMPION, BUT ALI LOOKED INTO THE EYES OF DUNDEE TO CONFIRM THE AWAITING DECISION. THAT PHOTOGRAPH TELLS THE WHOLE STORY OF THE FIGHT."
-THE FINAL VICTORY-

"THE BOXING LESSON"

"IF THERE EVER WAS A BOXING LESSON GIVEN TO AN INEXPERIENCED, CONFUSED HEAVYWEIGHT WHO WEIGHTS 201 POUNDS... YOU HAVE JUST SEEN IT."
CHRIS SCHENKEL — ABC SPORTS

"GORGEOUSLY SLOPPY"

"SLOPPY?" SAID A HAPPY ANGELO DUNDEE, THE MASTER TRAINER WHO PLOTTED ALI'S BATTLE PLAN. "IT WAS BEAUTIFULLY SLOPPY, WONDERFULLY SLOPPY, GORGEOUSLY SLOPPY, AND IT WAS THE ONLY DAMN WAY WE WERE GOING TO BEAT SPINKS."
-PAT PUTNAM-

"EXTRAORDINARY"

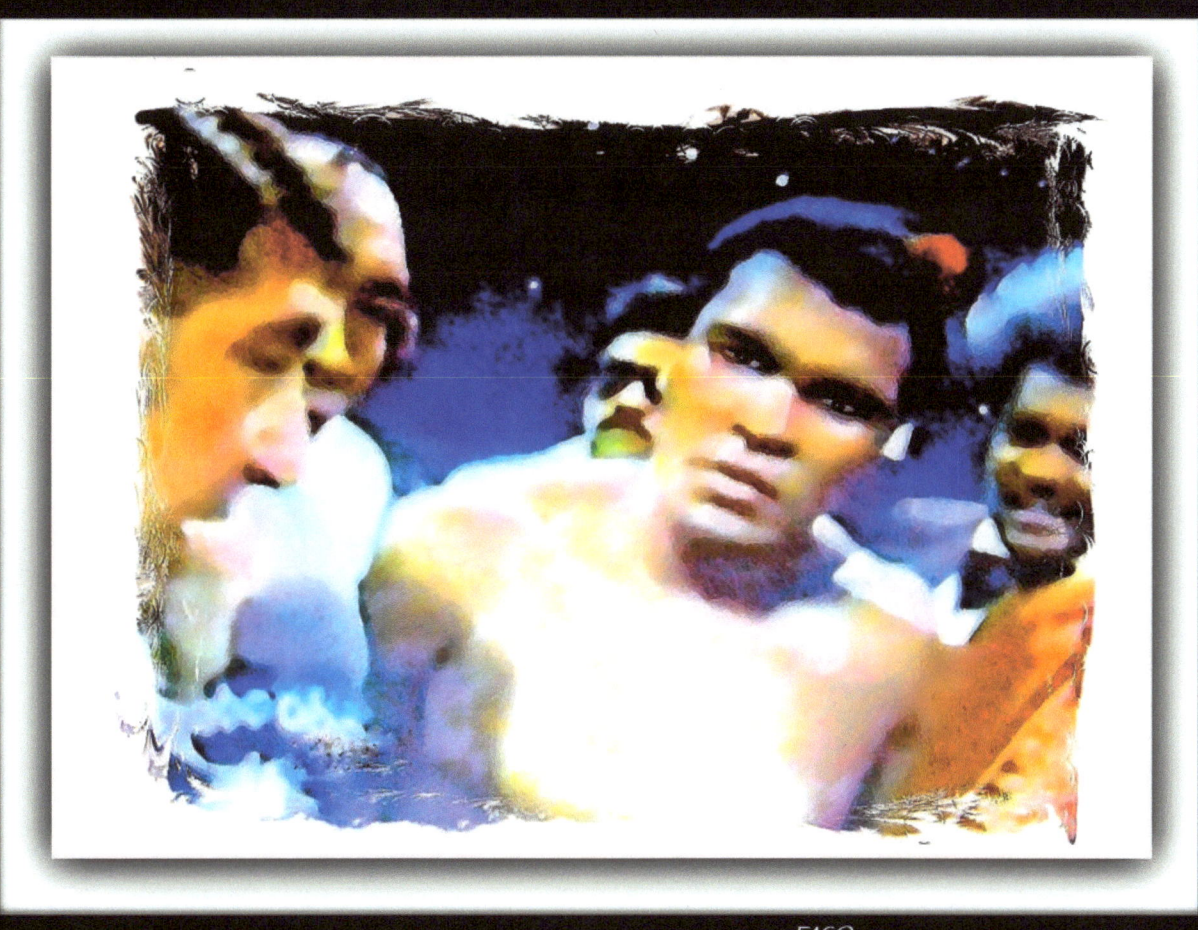

"IT HAS BEEN AN EXTRAORDINARY EVENING AS I HAVE EVER ENCOUNTERED...
THE WILDEST SCENES I HAVE EVER WITNESSED AND ON BALANCE,
ONE OF THE EXCEPTIONAL FIGHTS I HAVE EVER SEEN WAGED."
HOWARD COSELL – ABC SPORTS

"HE HAS BEEN A GIANT"

"ALI SAYS WHEN I LEAVE THIS FIGHT...
BOXING WILL BE A FORLORN THING —
HE IS PROBABLY RIGHT; HE HAS BEEN A GIANT."
HOWARD COSELL — ABC SPORTS

"THE CREATOR OF AN AGE"

"THE PROPHET, THE POET, THE PREACHER, THE PONTIFICATOR, THE PUGILIST...
THE GREATEST OF ALL TIME, HOW CAN YOU SAY HE ISN'T? THE CREATOR OF AN AGE."
CHRIS SCHENKEL — ABC SPORTS - RINGSIDE COMMENT AFTER FIGHT

"THE FINAL LEGACY"

FASO

THE UNPRECEDENTED THIRD HEAVYWEIGHT CHAMPIONSHIP TITLE WON BY MUHAMMAD ALI, HIS FINAL VICTORY, WILL STAND AS ONE THE GREATEST HUMAN ACHIEVEMENTS IN ALL OF SPORTING HISTORY.
"THE FINAL VICTORY"
PAUL LEO FASO

"IMPOSSIBLE"

"IMPOSSIBLE IS JUST A BIG WORD THROWN ABOUT BY SMALL MEN WHO FIND IT EASIER TO LIVE IN A WORLD THEY'VE BEEN GIVEN — THAN TO EXPLORE THE POWER THEY HAVE TO CHANGE IT. IMPOSSIBLE IS NOT A FACT. IT IS NOT A DECLARATION...IT'S A DARE — IMPOSSIBLE IS POTENTIAL. IMPOSSIBLE IS TEMPORARY — IMPOSSIBLE IS NOTHING."
-MUHAMMAD ALI-

"ALI TAUGHT US TO TRANSCEND"

"MUHAMMAD ALI TAUGHT US TO TRANSCEND MERE SOCIAL CATEGORIES AND
REPRESENTED THE HIGHEST LEVEL OF HUMAN BEING.
HIS ABILITY TO REWIRE WIDESPREAD ATTENTION INTO MASS THOUGHT
STILL REMAINS UNMATCHED."
CHUCK D – RAP ARTIST – FOUNDER OF PUBLIC ENEMY

"INTO HISTORY"

"JUDGING BY THE THUNDEROUS CROWD ERUPTION JUST AFTER
THE FINAL BELL — IT WAS ALL FOR ALI — WHEN THE FINAL DECISION
WAS ANNOUNCED, THERE WAS A WAVE OF HUMANITY THAT SURGED FORWARD, SURROUNDED
THE RING, OVERWHELMED SECURITY, THEN FINALLY SWEPT AN EXUBERANT
MUHAMMAD ALI OFF OF HIS FEET AND CARRIED HIM OUT — FOREVER INTO HISTORY."
"THE FINAL VICTORY"

"DREAMS COME TRUE"

FASO

"THE BEST WAY TO MAKE YOUR DREAMS COME TRUE IS TO WAKE UP."
-MUHAMMAD ALI-

"WE RISE AFTER WE FALL"

FASO

"SUCCESS IS NOT ACHIEVED BY WINNING ALL OF THE TIME. REAL SUCCESS COMES WHEN WE RISE AFTER WE FALL. SOME MOUNTAINS ARE HIGHER THAN OTHERS, SOME ROADS STEEPER THAN THE NEXT. THERE ARE HARDSHIPS AND SETBACKS BUT YOU CANNOT LET THEM STOP YOU. EVEN ON THE STEEPEST ROAD, YOU MUST NOT TURN BACK."
-MUHAMMAD ALI-

"70,000 PEOPLE SCREAMING"

"70,000 PEOPLE SCREAMING FOR MUHAMMAD ALI...
AND SO IT IS...HERE AT RINGSIDE...ASSUMING I AM STILL ON MIC...
AS MUHAMMAD ALI IS LED AWAY BY HIS CROWD AND LEON SPINKS
IN THE MOST GENTLEMANLY MANNER POSSIBLE, CONGRATULATED."
HOWARD COSELL – ABC SPORTS

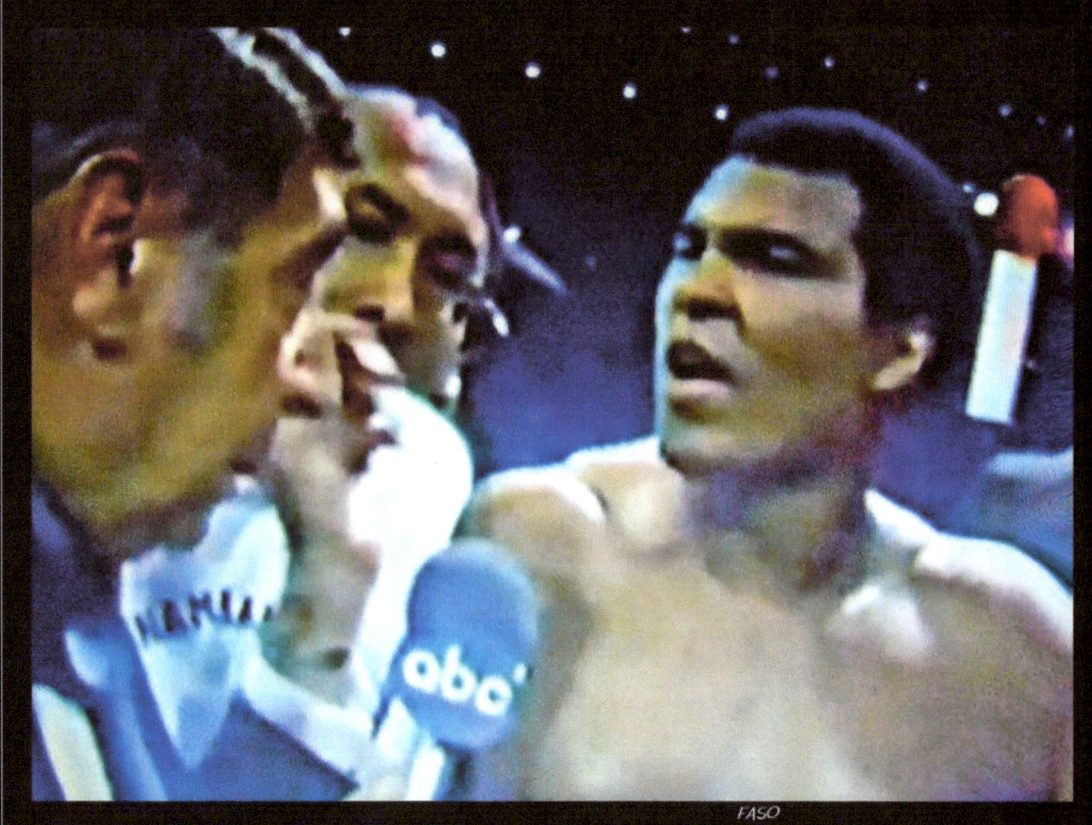

"YOU KNOW I'M BAD"

"I'VE WRESTLED WITH ALI GATORS. I'VE TUSSLED WITH A WHALE. I HAVE HANDCUFFED LIGHTNING AND THROWN THUNDER IN JAIL. YOU KNOW I AM BAD JUST LAST WEEK I MURDERED A ROCK, INJURED A STONE, HOSPITALIZED A BRICK. I'M SO MEAN I MAKE MEDICINE SICK." -MUHAMMAD ALI-

"DON'T QUIT"

"I HATED EVERY MINUTE OF TRAINING, BUT I SAID, DON'T QUIT. SUFFER NOW AND LIVE THE REST OF YOUR LIFE AS A CHAMPION."
MUHAMMAD ALI

"LIVE EVERYDAY"

"LIVE EVERYDAY AS IF IT WERE YOUR LAST BECAUSE SOME DAY… YOU'RE GOING TO BE RIGHT."
-MUHAMMAD ALI-

"BOTTOM OF HIS SOUL"

"ONLY A MAN WHO KNOWS WHAT IT IS LIKE TO BE DEFEATED CAN REACH DOWN TO THE BOTTOM OF HIS SOUL AND COME UP WITH THE EXTRA OUNCE OF POWER IT TAKES TO WIN WHEN THE MATCH IS EVEN."
MUHAMMAD ALI

"TAKE RISKS"

 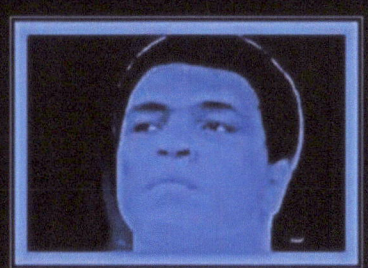 
 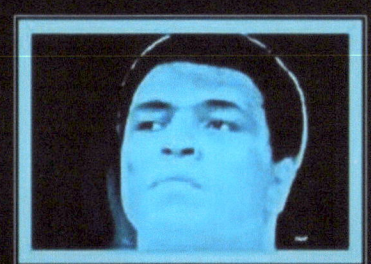 
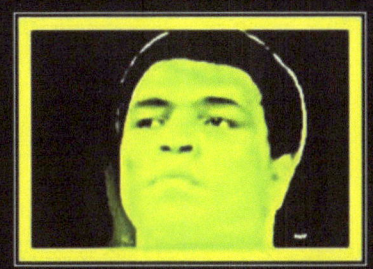  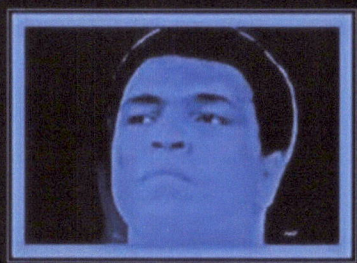

"HE WHO IS NOT COURAGEOUS ENOUGH TO TAKE RISKS WILL ACCOMPLISH NOTHING IN LIFE."
-MUHAMMAD ALI-

"NO WINGS"

"A MAN WHO HAS NO IMAGINATION HAS NO WINGS."
-MUHAMMAD ALI-

MUHAMMAD ALI

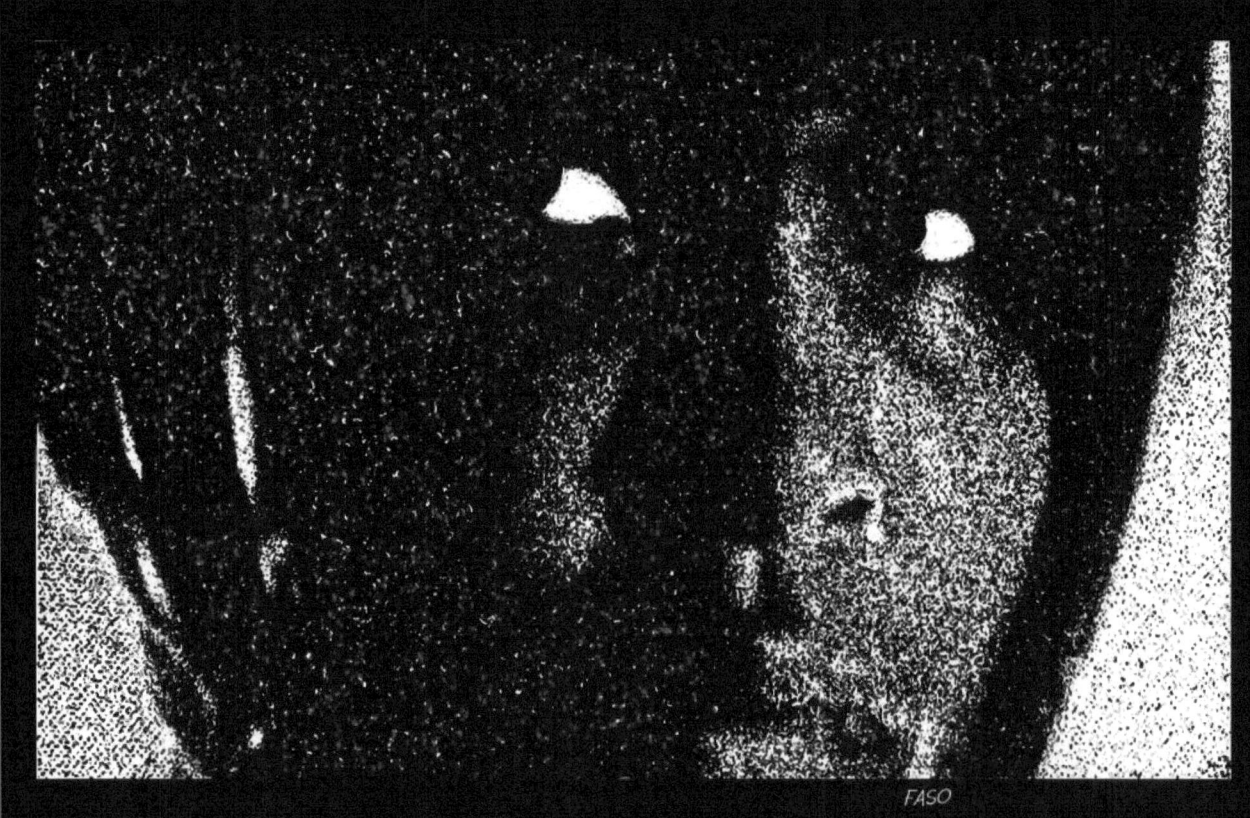

"THE HANDS CAN'T HIT
WHAT THE EYES CAN'T SEE."
MUHAMMAD ALI

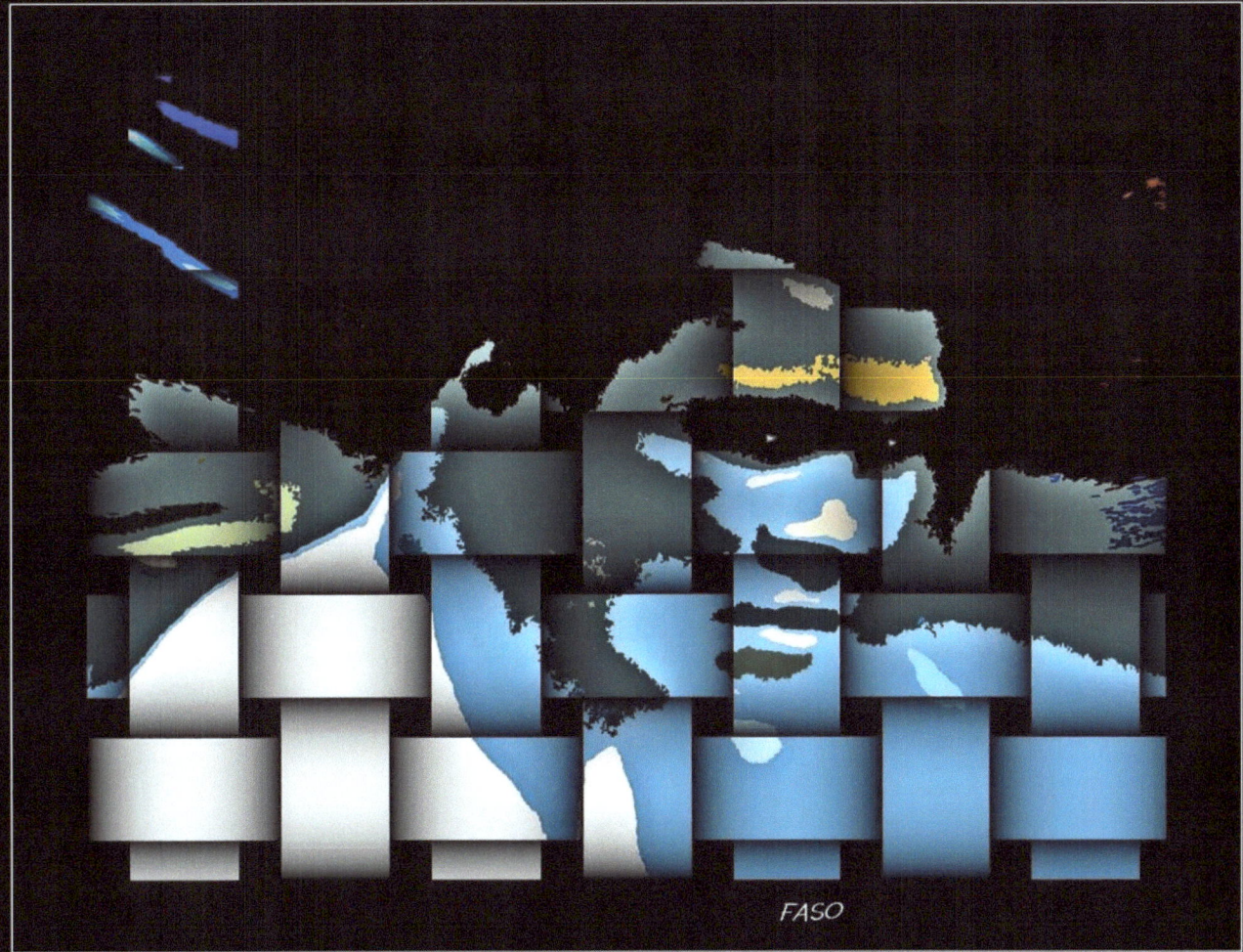

"ORDINARY MAN"

"I AM AN ORDINARY MAN WHO WORKED HARD TO DEVELOP THE TALENT I WAS GIVEN. I BELIEVED IN MYSELF AND I BELIEVE IN THE GOODNESS OF OTHERS."
-MUHAMMAD ALI-

"FRIENDSHIP"

"FRIENDSHIP IS THE HARDEST THING IN THE WORLD TO EXPLAIN...IT'S NOT SOMETHING YOU LEARN IN SCHOOL. BUT IF YOU HAVEN'T LEARNED THE MEANING OF FRIENDSHIP, YOU HAVEN'T LEARNED ANYTHING."
-MUHAMMAD ALI-

"HE'S BUDDHA - WALKING"

"ALI MEANS SO MUCH TO US — NO MATTER YOUR RELIGION OR COLOR — HE GRABS YOU — HE'S BUDDHA WALKING. THERE'S SOMETHING ABOUT HIM THAT IS SO PROFOUND AND LOVABLE. HE'S AN AMAZING GUY, AN AMAZING FORCE ON EARTH."
BILLY CRYSTAL – COMEDIAN

MUHAMMAD ALI
"I'M GONNA UPSET THE WORLD!"

FINAL THOUGHTS

THERE COULD BE NO GREATER TRIBUTE PAID TO MUHAMMAD ALI THAN THE MULTI MILLION DOLLAR ALI CENTER BUILT IN HIS HOMETOWN OF LOUISVILLE, KENTUCKY. THOSE INVOLVED WITH THAT ENDEAVOR HAVE PLACED SQUARELY IN FRONT OF THE WORLD, AN EVERLASTING LIVING HEARTBEAT OF A BELOVED AMERICAN LEGEND. THE CENTER WILL SERVE, NO DOUBT, AS A CALL TO ALL PEOPLE OF EVERY RACE AND CREED TO RISE ON EACH ONE'S OWN MERIT BY ASPIRING TO THOSE OUTSTANDING ACHIEVEMENTS MADE BY MUHAMMAD ALI. IN KEEPING WITH THE ALI CENTER'S MISSION TO CHERISH THE LIFE AND TIMES OF MUHAMMAD ALI, THIS BOOK WAS ASSEMBLED ALSO.

MY HOPE TO ALL;
THAT YOU WILL VIEW THE PHOTO/ART IN THIS BOOK, AS WELL AS THE E-BOOK AT AMAZON.COM AND MANY ONLINE VIDEOS POSTED ON THE INTERNET CAPTURING THE EXCITEMENT INSIDE THE SUPERDOME IN 1978. THEN LOOK BACK UPON MUHAMMAD ALI WITH RESPECT AND ADMIRATION, TO KNOW WHY HE IS AND ALWAYS WILL BE:
THE GREATEST HEAVYWEIGHT BOXER OF ALL TIME.

PAUL LEO FASO
WWW.THEFINALVICTORY.NET

PAUL LEO FASO
AMERICAN PHOTOGRAPHER

PAUL RECEIVED HIS BACHELOR OF ARTS DEGREE FROM THE STATE UNIVERSITY OF NEW YORK AT BUFFALO AFTER SERVING IN THE U.S. ARMY WITH THE 82ND AIRBORNE DIVISION.

DURING HIS CAREER, HE HAS BEEN ACTIVE IN PRODUCING, PROMOTING, AND MARKETING PHOTOGRAPHIC ART IN THE PAST FOUR DECADES, HE HAS PLACED HIS WORKS INTO CORPORATE AND GOVERNMENT ENVIRONMENTS THROUGHOUT THE NATION. CLIENTS HAVE RANGED FROM TURNER BROADCASTING TO HILTON HOTEL OPENINGS: PHOTO/ART DERIVATIVES WERE CREATED FROM THE BEATLES FIRST MULTI-MEDIA FILM "THE BEATLES- A WAY WITH WORDS". PAUL HAS ADDITIONALLY CREATED OVER 25,0000 FILM TRANSPARENCIES AS WELL AS OVER 250,000 DIGITAL IMAGES FOR LICENSE AND PUBLICATION.

HIS PHOTOGRAPHIC ARTWORK HAS BEEN UTILIZED BY BROADCAST, PUBLISHING & ADVERTISING INDUSTRIES AS WELL BY THE U.S. GOVERNMENT. UNDER THE AUTHORITY OF THE STATUE OF LIBERTY/ELLIS ISLAND FOUNDATION, INC. PAUL'S PHOTOGRAPHIC ART WAS EXCLUSIVELY LICENSED AS "THE OFFICIAL LIMITED EDITION" OF THE STATUE OF LIBERTY FOR THE CENTENNIAL IN 1986 AS DIRECTED BY PRESIDENT REAGAN. PAUL'S CORPORATION, PLF ENTERPRISES INC. RECEIVED A G.S.A. CONTRACT TO PRODUCE PHOTOGRAPHIC ART FOR U.S. GOVERNMENT BUILDINGS, HOSPITALS AND EMBASSIES. PAUL HAS LIVED IN ATLANTA AND THE PALM BEACH AREA FOR THE LAST 45 YEARS.

CREDITS

ABC WIDE WORLD OF SPORTS· ALI THEN AND NOW· THE LAST STARLET — NY MAGAZINE — SOUND AND FURY· SPORTS ILLUSTRATED — SILVER STAR MEDIA GROUP, INC. SOURCE INTERLINK MEDIA, LLC — TIME MGAZINE — YOU TUBE — MUHAMMAD ALI — RAHAMAN ALI — BUNDINI BROWN — HOWARD COSELL — CUS D'AMATO — OSCAR DELA HOYA — ANGELO DUNDEE — CHUCK "D" ROGER EBERT — JIMMY ELLIS — GEORGE FOREMAN — MICHAEL J. FOX — JOE FRAZIER — FRANK GIFFORD — LARRY HOLMES — KAREEM ABDUL JABBAR — MICHAEL JORDAN — BILLIE JEAN KING — DON KING — DAVE KINDRED — CHUCK "THE ICEMAN" LIDDELL — SONNY LISTON — DANNY LYON · ZIGGY MARLEY · LARRY MERCHANT — JOHN C. MERINGOLO — KEN NORTON — FERDIE PACHECHO — PAT PUTNAM — CHRIS SCHENKEL — WILL SMITH — SOCRATES — LEON SPINKS — SYLVESTER STALLONE — RICHARD STENGEL — TONY STEWART — BURT SUGAR — JOSE TORRES — MIKE TYSON — DANA WHITE — EDY WILLIAMS — JOSE TORRES — MIKE TYSON · DANA WHITE — EDY WILLIAMS — NORMAN MAILER — MARK KRAM — TUNNEY HUNSAKER — JAMES MICHENER — MAYA ANGELOU — THOMAS MEEKER · BILLY CRYSTAL — BILLY CONNOLLY —MARK COLLINS — SIR HENRY COOPER — RINGO STARR — PRESIDENT BARACK OBAMA · THE FINAL VICTORY

"CRITICISM IS EASY, ART IS DIFFICULT"
DESTOUCHES · 1732

"LIKE A BROTHER"

"I LOVE ALI LIKE A BROTHER AND LIKE A GUY THAT'S A CELEBRITY AND DONE A LOT FOR A LOT OF PEOPLE. ALI WAS ONE OF THOSE GUYS THAT MADE YOU FEEL GOOD ABOUT YOURSELF — HE MAKES EVERYONE FEEL GOOD...
LARRY HOLMES — HEAVYWEIGHT CHAMPION

"ALI ON ALI"

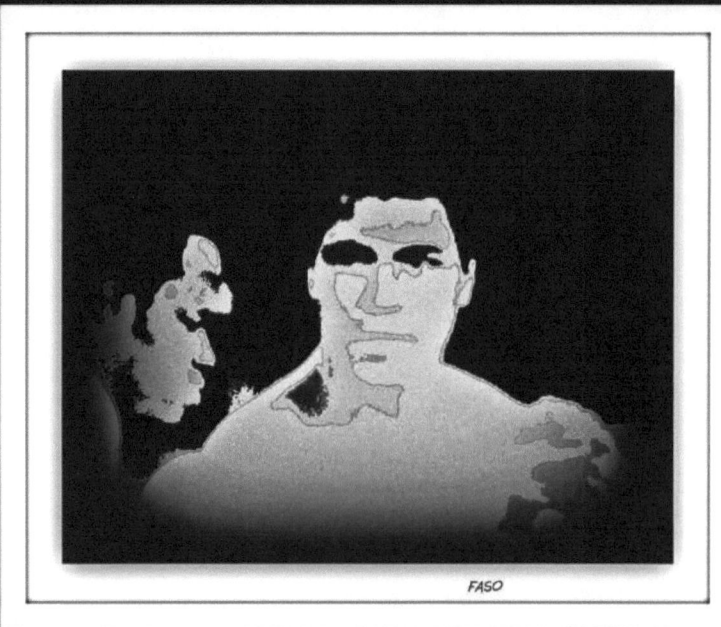

"HE TOOK A FEW CUPS OF LOVE, HE TOOK ONE TABLESPOON OF PATIENCE, ONE TEASPOON OF GENEROSITY, ONE PINT OF KINDNESS. HE TOOK ONE QUART OF LAUGHTER, ONE PINCH OF CONCERN AND THEN HE MIXED WILLINGNESS WITH HAPPINESS; HE ADDED LOTS OF FAITH AND HE STIRRED IT UP WELL. THEN HE SPREAD IT OVER THE SPAN OF A LIFETIME AND HE SERVED IT TO EACH AND EVERY DESERVING PERSON HE MET."

"I WISH YOU PEACE"

"ANY GREATNESS I HAVE ACHIEVED WAS MADE POSSIBLE BY MY BELIEF IN GOD, HARD WORK AND DETERMINATION AND A BELIEF IN MYSELF.
THE SAME CAN BE TRUE FOR YOU. I WISH YOU PEACE."
MUHAMMAD ALI

"NO CONTINENT, NO LANGUAGE, NO COLOR, NO OCEAN"

"MUHAMMAD ALI WAS NOT JUST MUHAMMAD ALI - THE GREATEST, THE AFRICAN-AMERICAN PUGILIST, HE BELONGED TO EVERYONE. THAT MEANS THAT HIS IMPACT RECOGNIZES NO CONTINENT, NO LANGUAGE, NO COLOR, NO OCEAN.
IT BELONGS TO US ALL, JUST AS MUHAMMAD ALI BELONGS TO US ALL"
- MAYA ANGELOU - POET

"KIND OF A PROPHET"

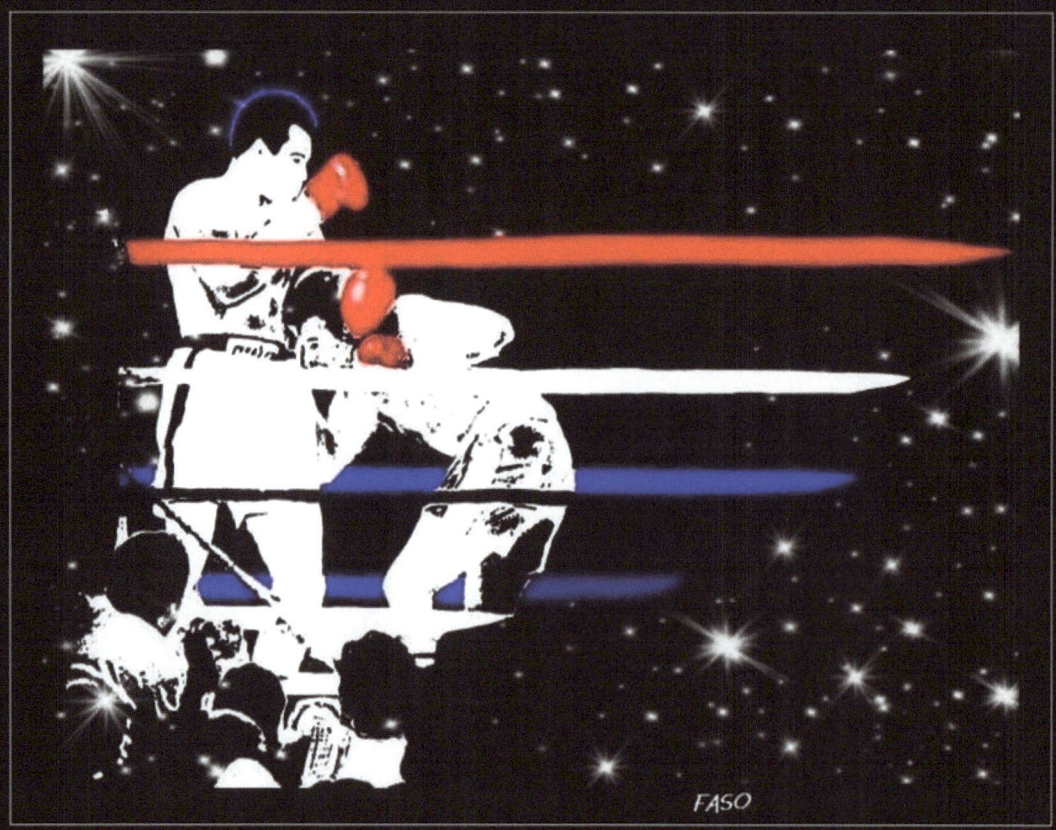

"MUHAMMAD ALI — A STRANGE KIND OF PHILOSOPHER, COMPLETELY ACCEPTABLE AND FUNNY. HE WAS THE BEST BOXER, A GREAT ATHLETE AND KIND OF A PROPHET IN A STRANGE WAY, ABOUT A NEW WORLD TO COME."
BILLY CONNELLY — MUHAMMAD ALI;
"THROUGH THE EYES OF THE WORLD" BY M. COLLINS

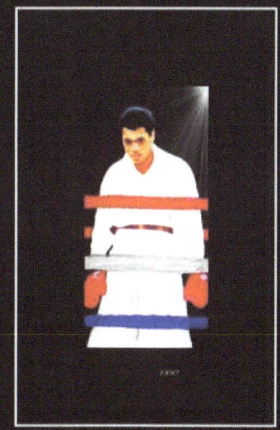

"ONE OF THE GREATEST THINGS THAT HAPPENED TO THE HUMAN RACE....
HAVING ALI AROUND."

ANGELO DUNDEE

www.ingramcontent.com/pod-product-compliance
Lightning Source LLC
Chambersburg PA
CBHW040533020526
44117CB00028B/15